THE WAY OF ASTROLOGY

✷

By IVY M. GOLDSTEIN - JACOBSON

✷

Member of

AMERICAN FEDERATION OF ASTROLOGERS

and

FIRST TEMPLE & COLLEGE OF ASTROLOGY

at Los Angeles

Engravings by Marge J. Zander

Author of

Mathematics of the Astrological Chart
Here and There in Astrology
Foundation of the Astrological Chart
The Dark Moon Lilith in Astrology
Simplified Horary Astrology
The Turn of a Lifetime Astrologically
All Over the Earth Astrologically

Photographed from Mrs. Jacobson's typing
and
Printed in the United States
by
Pasadena Lithographers
Pasadena, California

To my sister Heléne

for auld lang syne

Table of Contents

Subject   Page

CHARTS listed on page iv

Table of Contents

* * * * *

Introduction

There are those who, in the pursuit of knowledge
that may lead to understanding in diverse fields of
endeavor, fail to recognize that the most rewarding
search of all lies in the study of man himself. In
the beginning our greatest concern was not for what
was around us, but what was within us -- our reason
for being. In those days, man walked & talked with
God as the prophets did, the astrologers of the Old
Testament who studied the stars in their courses so
that Daniel answered Nebuchadnezzar correctly, Jos-
eph answered the Pharaoh, & Deborah led the army to
victory, to remember only a few. Those forecasters
are long gone, but they showed us the way and it is

THE WAY OF ASTROLOGY

What is man? Why does he behave as he does, and
why does he love, hate, fear, strive to succeed and
at last, die? What did he bring with him at birth,
how did he use it while here, and what will he take
with him at death? How can he know when to act and
when to wait, or say when events will come to pass?

His chart tells him his whole story, that he may
learn to read and be prepared. His planets tell him
what he is, why he is bound & what he is bound for;
their progressed aspects tell him what to expect as
well as when to expect it. All this and more also.

Besides finding out about himself, modern man is
interested in world affairs using the Ingress Chart,
people of importance to him by reading natal charts,
& answers to his questions by reading horary charts.
Read on and see.

Ivy M. Goldstein-Jacobson

THE WAY IT WAS WRITTEN

T H E   W A Y   I T   W A S   W R I T T E N

Astrology is the practical science of astronomy,
the latter being "up in the air" so to speak - with
astrology not only bringing it down to earth so man
can make practical use of the scientific facts, but
bringing it down long before astronomy as such came
into being. Ancient civilizations, and especially
those arising in Egypt, Babylon & Mesopotamia, etc.
recorded inscriptions that man finds today that are
many thousand years old but still decipherable, and
from those undying words we gain astrological lore.

Written on papyrus

In Egypt the writings were on papyrus, made from
a plant of that name, our first "paper" but unfortunately perishable because of its vegetable nature.
The Greeks also used papyrus, most of such writings
perishing along with those of the Egyptians.   But
they had something else that did endure, telling us
much of what had been written on papyrus - and this
was due to the custom in both of these countries of
carving hieroglyphics on the stone walls that lined
the rooms in which the papyrus writings were stored
as a sort of reference system or "wall-index" which
told about the contents of the different scrolls to
enable the priests to find the desired work easily.
Today's seekers of knowledge may not know the whole
story but we know in part - because of that literal
"hand-writing on the wall", an actual Rock of Ages.

Written on clay

In Mesopotamia & Babylon adobe-like clay tablets
were used, similar in a way to the adobe bricks of
our Western States. Their writing was done with an
instrument called a stylus. They also endured thru
the thousands of years that have passed, & like the
years the tablets too are numbered in the thousands
giving us a priceless record of our long-ago yester-
days. They include the Tel el Amarna letters found
in 1887 by a peasant woman, and they consist of 350
tablets written between 1411/1358 BC, & are letters
in Babylonian script from princes to Egyptian kings.

In the main, all of these were of historical, political & meteorological import: they told of wars,
men of significance, rulers & countries, the flood-
ing of the Nile, and so on. They are without great
astrological influence on mankind today except insofar as their dynasty-dating provides an opportunity
for astronomers to fix the planet positions at that
time, giving us the aspects that prove we are today
as we were then, for it is moreover still true that
there is nothing new under the Sun (Ecclesias. 1:9).

Written on parchment

The writings that did give us invaluable astrological light are those of the ancient astrologers,
the Hebrew prophets of the Old Testament: they also
gave us the symbols for the Signs and the Sun, Moon,
Saturn, Jupiter, Mars, Venus & Mercury. The figure
that stands out most prominently is that of Isaiah,
the first of the prophets, from whose very hand we
have the very book (scroll) he wrote 2675 years ago;
imperishable words written on a scroll among those
whose recent discovery is known the world around --
and the accuracy of his prophecies is well proven.

Though nomadic, the tribes were an intellectual people given to writing "books" which in their wanderings had to be easily portable & light in weight. They used sheepskin which they treated and polished to smoothness with volcanic or lava stone now known as pumice, resulting in a very-long-lived parchment. A diploma today is often on parchment & facetiously referred to as a sheepskin and presented rolled, as a "scroll". The Hebrew writings were rolled around sticks in a single long roll, wrapped in fine linen and placed for safe-keeping in pottery jars called keli-cheres, designed for that special purpose with dome-shaped lids - then stored in the deep recesses of nearby caves. Those dome-shaped lids are today memorialized in the roof-design of the building in Jerusalem called THE SHRINE OF THE BOOK wherein the Dead Sea Scrolls are kept; of these we speak of the Scroll of Isaiah & note that he writes of things to come as though they had already happened and things in the past as though they were still to take place.

Written in stone

In Isaiah 19:19 it is foretold that "There shall be an altar in Egypt in the midst of the land - and at the border thereof", recognized now as the Great Pyramid of Ghizeh. It stands directly in the midst of the land of Egypt & also directly on the borderline that separates Upper & Lower Egypt, fulfilling the description exactly. And not only is it in the midst of that land; it is in the exact midst of all the land surface of the whole earth -- as proven by its meridian and horizon circles dividing the globe into four equal sections, each containing the same amount of land. The Architect decided this center when the rest of the earth was unknown to the building Egyptians; something to think about, is it not?

The Great Pyramid of Ghizeh

Built by Cheops some 4500 years ago and covering
a base of over 13 acres, the Pyramid is unique, not
only in its tremendous size as well as centralized
site, but different besides from any other pyramid,
since it was never intended to be a tomb nor has it
ever been used as such; to all intents and purposes
it is what Isaiah called it - an altar whose mathematical relationship of one part to another exactly
reveals dates of historical events in both past and
future, as seen in Rutherford's books on pyramidol-
ogy. The Old Testament names two kinds of altars:
one for worship and one for a witness to the design
of the Deity. This one is a mathematical witness,
"measuring out & declaring the end thereof" in timing & foretelling. Its astrological value to us is
that it led to the then-unknown Greenwich Meridian.

The Pyramid uses a "distance basis" of one cubit
inch to one solar year, measured along passages inside the Pyramid to recesses, chambers, steps, etc.
there, to ascertain event dates with remarkable exactitude. It was begun in 2613 B.C. & completed in
2589 B.C. according to the reign of Cheops (Khufu).
Its DESCENDING passage refers to still earlier B.C.
for time measurement marking 5394 B.C. for the cre-
ation of Adam - or what is more reasonable, the beginning of the Adamic Age, thousands of years after
the age of the Neanderthal Man. The ASCENDING passage dates A.D. onward, ending with 2994 A.D. which
is a date for the reader to hold in mind as we proceed further toward the next "writing" to be read.

With the building of the Great Pyramid the world
entered its various periods of great civilizations
embracing differing trends of political & religious
beliefs that marked time until the beginning of the
New Age in which we find ourselves. Like all ages,

it began with the Vernal Equinox: that was when the
arc O-Aries of the Vernal Equinox rested on the Pyramid like the Ark on Mt. Ararat, presaging a change
to a new center that was still to be reached by the
next Vernal Equinox O-Aries and would be recognized
by an observatory built without reference to longitude and latitude, these not having been established.
At that distant time the Pyramid would no longer be
taken as the center of the earth, nor would we deal
with cubit measurement any more in forecasting, but
with astrological charts and the planetary aspects.

The Greenwich Observatory

The Greenwich Observatory was built in 1675 A.D.
the longitude 00:00 not being set until 1884.   In
1948 all astronomical work was transferred from the
observatory to Herstmonceux but the location of the
Prime Meridian 00:00 remained unchanged at what was
then re-named Flamsteed House for the first Astron-
omer Royal, Sir John Flamsteed, & as late as 1960 it
was opened as a museum by Her Majesty Elizabeth II.

Geographical & astronomical work both arise from
the same Greenwich point, the Prime Meridian 00:00.
From there, Standard Time is reckoned & the planet-
places calculated for the ephemeris & it is the Sun
in his pathway or Ecliptic that is our prime mover.
The twelve Signs lie along his pathway and he has a
lesser and a greater cycle there. The lesser is his
Mean Solar Year of 365 days beginning with & returning to the Vernal Equinox O-Aries around March 21st
each year at the rate of $00°59'08''$ per day, thus we
always know which Sign he is in during a Solar Year.
As stated in Ezekiel 4:5 and 4:6, one day's rate is
also taken as a year's rate in progressing a chart,
which can be more than 90 days in the ephemeris; or
past 100 days for one hoping to live over 100 years.

The Great Sidereal Cycle

For progress through great ages, however, we use
the Great Sidereal Year because of its vast cycle,
28,174 years, with its aeonic revelations when over
first the Great Pyramid and later the Greenwich Meridian; thus we have the distance between these two
to equate with time.   Records of ancient Memphis,
now Cairo (ten miles from the Pyramid), give us the
Vernal Equinox 0-Aries there in 2978 B.C., the date
that leads us to the time when it would be over the
location of the then-unknown 0° Greenwich Meridian.
From that date we can discover, by way of the Great
Sidereal Cycle, our place today in the great scheme.

The Great Sidereal Cycle 28,174 years measures 2348
years in one Sign, therefore 78 years in one degree
and we note that as it moves forward thru the years
it moves backward thru the Signs as Aries to Pisces
and this is known as the precession of the equinox.
By the time 0-Aries reached the Greenwich Meridian,
the Sign behind it, Pisces, would be on the Pyramid.

The longitude of the Pyramid, our starting-point,
is 31°10' east of Greenwich but as we are using the
ecliptic which is oblique by 23°27' we find according to Johndro's calculations on p. 12 of his EARTH
IN THE HEAVENS that the equated distance is 33°24',
or 3°24' more than one Sign between the two places.
1° = 78 years, so 3° = 234 years; 24/60' x 78 = 31
years or 265 years to add to 2348 years in one Sign
or 2613 years' equated distance between the places.

        2978 B.C. 0-Aries over the Pyramid
     - 2613 equated distance to Greenwich
        365 B.C. 0-Aries on Greenwich M.C.

The reason we subtract is because the years B.C.
decrease as they approach 1 A.D. and then increase.

Our place in the scheme of things

On page 8 we noted 2994 A.D. as the end of the
ascending passage in the Pyramid. It signifies the
end of the 1000-year millenium which thus begins in
1994 A.D. only 27 years away from this year 1967 before which millenium we will enter the Aquarian Age
in which we hope to establish "Peace on Earth" thru
the Brotherhood of Man, as represented by Aquarius.
We are at present still in the Piscean Age of bond-
age, bigotry & man's inhumanity to his brother man.

Since the Vernal Equinox moves backward thru the
Signs, Aries 0 Retrograde is the same as Pisces 30R
which we now employ for greater clarity as follows:

          2348 years retrograde in any Sign
    -      365 B.C. Pisces 30R on Greenwich
          1983 A.D. Aquar. 30R on Greenwich
    -     1967 A.D. the year we are now in
            16 years' wait for Aquarian Age

This means that during the next 16 years we must
recognize that all men are free and equal if we are
to enter the millenium in 1994 although it may take
that 1000 years before the end of the Millenium for
the world-wide accomplishment of that Great Scheme.
The struggle now in progress by minority groups all
over the world must ultimately achieve the promised
Utopian goal toward which the ascending passage in
the Great Pyramid of Ghizeh reaches its end in 2994.

From writings on papyrus and clay, hieroglyphics on
stone, prophecies on parchment, cubit measurement in
the Pyramid to the Observatory at Greenwich, thence
to the planets we can read today, we now understand
our place in the Scheme and the way it was written.

✷ ✷ ✷ ✷ ✷

THE WAY OF A NATAL CHART

READING YOUR NATAL CHART

As you study this section, set down the descrip-
tions that tally with the Midheaven, Ascendant and
planets in your natal chart. This gives an outline
of the characteristics you were born with that make
up your personal and individual pattern, different
from that of others born on the same date and it is
yours for life. It reveals what your future is to
be as it unfolds and develops along with your chart.
These are questions you want answered, and it is of
small moment to wonder unless you know how to read.

Arrangement of planets

With your chart before you, the first thing that
you notice is the disposition of planets around the
wheel, giving the first clue to your mode of action
in life. Are they standing alone & thus dispersed,
or coupled in pairs, or in groups of three or more?

When scattered about the wheel it means that you
have an embarrassment of interests - too many irons
in the fire - attracted too readily to a new interest because there is little time-lapse between them
as to spacing. The interests you like best however
and will return to are shown by the planets square
the Ascendant zodiacally or square the 1st House by
being in the 10th or 4th House which is a "mundane"
aspect (by house only). Why the square? Because
it is the most forceful of all aspects, demanding a
dynamic response similar to the nature of Mars, who
is the most energetic & resourceful planet we have.
You always make your best effort under the squares.
You would say that here is a person of diversified,
long-range interests but also selective by squares.

Planets standing alone, especially the Sun, Moon
or the planet ruling the Sign on the Ascendant show
that you work best alone and can forge your own way
in life, independent of others, particularly in the
matters ruled by the houses they are in. This is a
passing clue, also, to your early life - disclosing
that you were left largely to your own devices as a
child, denied ordinary cooperation & companionship.
You got along well by yourself then and you do now.

Planets in pairs show reliance on another person
and it will bear fruit if in good aspect zodiacally
to the Ascendant or mundanely to the 1st House - as
from any house but the 6th, 7th or 8th which are in
mundane quincunx or opposition to the 1st. You get
no cooperation from an opposition: the other person
pulls away or holds back and you are fully aware of
his disinterest because this is a Full Moon type of
aspect: it makes everything as clear as day to you.

The quincunx forces you to reorganize your aim &
settle for less, or assume unwanted responsibility.
Any good aspect makes you expect great things - but
if opposition or quincunx by HOUSE you accept less.

Planets in groups of three or more give related,
attainable goals; interests that can be reached and
easily if in good zodiacal or mundane aspect to the
1st House. The square means great self-application
with ultimate success: the opposition baffles you &
the quincunx attains in part but also exacts a tax.

The most concentrated effort on your part comes
from having planets concentrated in a quadrant, and
this allows you to concentrate your attention where
you can specialize toward a certain goal.   When on
the Ascendant side of the chart it is more personal
in nature; on the Descendant side, more impersonal;
in either case, the specialization assures success.

The majority of planets above the horizon allows
a larger scope of interests on a wider plane & more
likely to attract attention to those interests than
when below the horizon in the less-brilliant sphere
of activity, that being the dark half of the chart.
You are more outgoing and much easier to understand.
The majority below the horizon narrows the scope of
interests to those attracting less outer attention:
you are less outgoing and much harder to understand.

Planets in angular houses are definite & active,
their characteristics more noticeable in your appearance & demeanor, and their power surer to bring
you publicity. In succeedent houses you work quiet-
ly but persistently and with less publicity - still
less in cadent houses, working behind the scenes so
to speak & achieving your renown from within walls.

Natal planets are always stronger when placed in
the Signs or Houses they rule naturally, where they
thus have prominence that gives you higher standing
in life because of their dignity plus the attention
you command in the matters signified by that house.
Your planets have ACCIDENTAL DIGNITY in any angular
house whether they rule it or not, the more so when
in the 10th of superior standing and public respect.

A planet in its natural house or Sign by mutual
reception with another PLANET gives exchange status
revealing that you have dual capabilities & will be
aided in expressing them by someone else: it always
brings changes for the better in life, and will get
you out of whatever scrape you get into. Reception
by HOUSE operates if each of two planets rules the
Sign on the cusp of the house the other is in, giving delegated authority to act for one another and
assume the management or responsibility temporarily.
It frequently works in a semi-adoptive capacity, so
that a friendship can become a foster relationship.

The restless significators are the Moon, Uranus,
Mercury and Mars: the Cardinal Signs Aries, Cancer,
Libra and Capricorn: the Mutable (adaptable to persuasion) Signs Gemini, Virgo, Sagittarius & Pisces:
the angular houses (1st, 7th, 4th, 10th) and cadent
houses (3rd, 9th, 6th, 12th). Any of these planets
or Signs or houses prominent in your chart reveals
restlessness, with many changes in life and address.

The placid significators are Jupiter, Venus, the
Sun, Saturn, Neptune and probably the stolid Pluto;
the Fixed Signs Taurus, Leo, Scorpio, Aquarius: and
the succeedent houses (2nd, 5th, 8th & 11th).   Any
of these prominent in your chart describes you as a
quieter, more settled person disliking much change.

Your chart may perhaps combine the foregoing, in
which case you may be quiet, retiring and averse to
making major changes, but at the same time given to
attracting publicity & changes due to circumstances
otherwise evident in the chart. Or the same contra-
diction in reverse may be shown - with restlessness
and chafing at environmental restriction and denial
of the opportunity for public life that is offered.

Rulers of the mental attributes

Mercury rules the conscious, logical, reasoning,
analytical and inquisitive mind expressed in words.
The Moon rules the subconscious, sensitive, changeable & emotional mind.   The unconscious mind ruled
by the spiritual planet Neptune gives extra-sensory
perception.   Uranus rules the inventive mind, new-
ness in ideas & the capacity to have the answer before the question is asked. Mars is the scientific
mind expressed in mathematics and mechanics.   Saturn rules the narrow & coldly judicial mind. Venus
is the artistic, romantic, contented mind. Jupiter
is the understanding, academic, philosophical mind.

The Ascendant

The Ascendant and the planet that rules the Sign on the 1st cusp govern your Temperament: a blending of the physical & mental. Where you find that ruler by Sign and house you are described temperamentally although any planet in the 1st House is to the fore and will modify your temperament by its own nature. A planet conjunct the Ascendant from the 12th-House side also colors your temperament & your outlook on life, while the number of degrees between them discloses your age when you first begin to reflect it.

The Sign on your Ascendant describes your nature and appearance in general, but the decanate reveals great hidden influence there, especially when Fixed because Fixed Signs ESTABLISH traits, conditions, & demand-for-fulfillment, whether the rising Sign itself be Cardinal or Mutable. What is fixed becomes inescapable: you would say that here is a person in line for a certain and definite future that will be to his advantage if the ruler of the 1st cusp is in good aspect to it or to Jupiter, Venus or Fortuna - and how he will attain it will be shown by planets in trine, sextile or square the Ascendant making it come without effort, by opportunity if grasped, or by dint of arduous self-application to his purpose.

Cardinal Signs & decanates are starters having a latent resolve to get somewhere in life, which they usually do earlier than most. Common Signs rising make many false starts but if the decanate is fixed they eventually attain success in life. They adapt to circumstances. Common decanates are very clever in adjusting to pressure & getting around obstacles or frustrations, thus they usually succeed in life. Fixed Signs rising take root early in life and win. If Aries is not rising, the Sign on the 1st belongs on a natural house that greatly affects the native.

The Sun and the Moon

The Sun represents your ego or Individuality and
the Moon your emotional nature or Personality which
is the outward expression that masks the inner ego;
the way you "project" your Self to others. Some of
us succeed by high, detached position in life, like
the Sun, and are considered personages. Some of us
succeed through closer, intimate contacts as by the
Moon & are called personalities. It is like a fav-
orite entertainer on the stage, a great personality
projecting charm that captivates the distinguished,
detached great personage who occupies the royal box.

The Sun above the horizon makes you a recognized
individualist, which is also true of the Sun in any
angular house: you decide your course for yourself.
Below the horizon and not in the 1st or 4th denotes
one whose course is likely to be decided by others.

The Moon above the horizon brings your personality out in the open, as it does also in any angular
house; you attract attention by personal magnetism.
Below the horizon and not in the 1st or 4th denotes
a more self-effacing personality avoiding attention.

It is important to understand that the Sun makes
the rules and the Moon carries them out, not unlike
the father and mother (theoretically, at least) and
his rule becomes your fate. He is the authority in
deciding your role in life while the Moon possesses
delegated authority from him to act in his name and
circle the wheel to contact each planet by arranged
aspect in orderly fashion and collect the facts you
need in playing the role his house-position denotes.

Always note the latitude of the Moon at birth, &
the closer it is to 5° 18' which is her greatest distance.   The closer her latitude, the more latitude

or leeway you take in handling matters having to do
with your role in life, the more freedom you assume
in your own name and the more self-reliant you are.

Your Sun throws light on the house he is in, and
that is the department of life where you shine best
and are intended to radiate out according to whatever that house represents. You are an authority &
a leader there, and recognized as such; you have an
inner consciousness of assurance in that department,
& your main role in life is dictated by that house.

The Moon by house position shows where you labor
to accomplish what your Individuality designates, &
since the Moon is magnetic she attracts to you what
that house contains for her use in serving the Sun.
It will be something related to his house-position.

Let us say that your Sun is in the 3rd House and
thus you are in the department of communication and
teaching: you feel at home in these matters and are
sure to express yourself (radiate out) accordingly.
Let us say, also, that your Moon is in the 8th, 6th
or 12th House, all of which lead in research power:
you will attract to yourself by 8th-House investigation, 6th-House analysis or 12th House-psychic apprehension the FACTS to suit the 3rd-House purpose.

The Signs the Sun & Moon are in at birth are the
channels through which they operate best, and if in
mutual reception anywhere in the chart (two in each
other's natural Sign) there is a diversity of abil-
ities - you have more than one avenue of expression
in life in more than one department where you could
be a Sun authority or Moon delegated-authority, because mutual receptions denote exchange status that
permits a planet to be also read as though back in
its own Sign in the house where its degree puts it.
Show such Sun & Moon symbols where they also work.

The Moon will be between two planets (or the Sun and a planet) no matter how far apart. The one she last passed over was before your birth and it shows what you built into your consciousness then for use now in fulfilling your Sun-pattern. It also shows by its nature how you approach any changes of plans or circumstances in life. Uranus for example would build-in radical interests along scientific lines & would also approach changes in general in a radical and independent manner, with a degree of immediacy. Saturn on the other hand would build-in practical & material interests, and would approach changes from a time-tested, practical standpoint & without haste.

The planet the Moon first passes over after your birth is the key that unlocks your Sun-pattern, and in the infant it generally shows by its nature what the child first reaches out for when given a choice of interests, as a book, a toy, a tool, a box, etc. Thus the future could be along literary lines, art, commerce, mechanics or a profession in such a case.

Since the Moon is intent on serving the Sun well, thereby looking out for your best interests, always give preference to the positive or well-intentioned keywords for the planets she contacts in his behalf. If conjunct or in good aspect, expect ease in reaching your goal. A bad aspect involves more effort & some obstacle in your way, & especially the square.

The Sun and Moon are the most dependable members of the celestial family because they are always direct in motion, moving forward to time results that will surely transpire. Planets direct at birth may promise future developments by applying to aspects, then break their promise by turning retrograde. We look ahead in the natal ephemeris 90 days or so and revise our expectations accordingly. The house the planet turns in tells the reason for such reneging.

Always note the houses carrying the Signs Cancer
and Leo for the things promised by the Moon and Sun
that will surely arrive in due time. If the Lights
are fortified by good placement or good aspects the
promise will be fulfilled in greater substance; but
even if not so fortified some gain will be granted;
all the earlier if the Lights are above the horizon
or in the 1st House: everything comes to you there.

The Sun or Moon in or ruling the 1st will always
bring personal action and personal gain.   The 2nd,
money and substance in general.   The 3rd, learning:
although the Moon belittles it & resents the method.
The 4th, gain through real estate and inheritance.
The 5th, through creative work, wagers, the father,
& a good child.   The 6th, through voluntary service
& especially where you find the ruler of that house.
The 7th, through partnership, marriage, contracts &
changing to a better location.   The 8th, by legacy,
settlement, marriage, social security and presents.
The 9th, by publishing, teaching, foreign import or
export, insurance policies & dealing with strangers.
The 10th, action involving the career: the Sun will
strengthen it, the Moon there usually abandons what
was first begun in favor of another approach.   The
11th, gain through friends, memberships, adoptions,
great expectations if the ruler of the 2nd is well-
fortified (the 2nd being the way the 11th will end)
& through fortuitous circumstances if the ruler of
the 11th is in good house-aspect to the 11th cusp.
The 12th, by institutional means, help in adversity
or gain by working in seclusion to reach your goal.

If the Sun, Moon or ruler of the Ascendant is in
an intercepted Sign there will be interference or a
delay in getting started in life.   An intercepted
Sign alone shows interference in the affairs there.
The Sun, Moon or ruler of the Ascendant progressing
into such a Sign seeks seclusion for a good reason.

The Planets

The houses that will be mainly active in developing your pattern in life will be those tenanted by planets at birth because these are forces of action that are stimulated over and over again by the Moon and other progressions and major transits aspecting them. Aspects galvanize planets into operation and these respond according to their nature & regarding the matters of the houses they are in: effortlessly if they are placid planets in good aspect elsewhere but with greater effort if they are energetic & in aspect elsewhere. The square is the most activating.

Planets in aspect to the Ascendant, its ruler or a planet in the 1st House, whether at birth, by progression or heavy transit singling them out, always directly involve the person whose chart it is. Progressions & transits that do not aspect the Ascendant, its ruler or a planet in the 1st House signify activity in your circle affecting other persons and house-matters that you hear about sooner or later - but you yourself are not necessarily much involved. In passing, we remember that we are always directly involved when the Ascendant or its ruler or a planet in the 1st House at birth progresses to aspects.

Planets always retain their interest in whatever is ruled by the houses they are in at birth besides their added interest in the matters of the house in which they are temporarily posited by progression. If from there they aspect the Ascendant, etc., such interest becomes personally active and if aspecting the Sun or Moon also it will further the life-work. If they conjunct a planet by such progression, they receive some equipment or knowledge or benefit from some new acquaintance, which also helps the career.

A planet's progressed aspect generally registers most at the time the month-by-month Moon aspects it.

The retrograde condition

It is this writer's observation of planets retrograde at birth that they represent persons ruled by
the houses they are in who break promises they make
to the one whose chart it is or withhold for a time
something that belongs to him. Neither are they to
be depended on completely in hastening the success,
because they delay what the house otherwise offers.

Each house rests on the one immediately below it.
The career-10th depends for success on the 11th-of-
circumstances in life; a retrograde planet there at
birth will delay but not deny any promised success.
A square to it only inspires it to greater effort.

It is also observed that such retrograde planets
represent persons of the house they are in who will
become separated from the native and thus alienated
to greater or lesser extent, the more enduring when
in Fixed Signs. If the ruler of the Ascendant goes
retrograde after birth, the native deliberately re-
linquishes family ties and customs for the duration
of the condition which may endure for life; but not
with Leo or Cancer on the Ascendant, the rulers Sun
& Moon, always direct, never abandoning the family.

If the retrograde planet is a malefic it reveals
that a person of the house it is in is unfortunate,
may have been put out of the house or family circle
or may even suffer exile. If aspecting the Ascendant, its ruler or a planet in the 1st, the misfortune may involve someone near or dear to the native.

As you study the following pages for the planets
in thumb-nail description, note that they are fully
treated in this writer's HERE & THERE IN ASTROLOGY,
pages 3-47; also in her SIMPLIFIED HORARY ASTROLOGY
pages 55 thru 63, equally applicable to natal work.

SATURN and JUPITER

SATURN'S symbol ♄ is that of the flail or plow-
share, that which beats out the chaff and brings to
practical usage that which is best in us. Where he
is placed by house, there do we extract the best in
life, abjuring frivolity in favor of profundity and
down-to-earth self-application as though digging in
the depths for what will be useful to us - like the
farmer & lover of the soil that he is. In the 2nd,
3rd or 4th House he builds up an estate in time and
leaves something of value to posterity. His symbol
and Jupiter's are also in reverse (♄ ♃) so that
his reaches down into earthy matter while Jupiter's
symbol, the celestial harp, reaches up to spiritual
realms of higher thought; academic & philosophical,
occult matters and indulgence toward human frailty,
being the Greater Benefic. Where Jupiter is placed
you are greatly rewarded, recompensed for any loss,
most law-abiding & honest and able to point the way.
Where Saturn is placed you earn your reward, but it
endures as part of you through future incarnations.

Saturn is serious and concise in speech, thrifty in
all things, saving for future use, liking seclusion;
where Jupiter is loquacious, optimistic, generous &
warmly friendly, with a capacity to let go freely &
enjoy himself; where Saturn never gives up nor lets
go, always keeping a string attached so that a hold
or grasp is always evident. When he rules or is in
the 7th he is a quiet, rather humble mate, spending
only for the family, self-denying & self-abnegating
and finding it difficult to demonstrate affection.
He rules shade and darkness: in any cadent house he
"draws the shade" over something or someone related
to the adjoining angular house because he is behind
it in a secretive 12th-House relationship. When he
rules the 8th cusp he causes very serious accidents
if the Ascendant squares a malefic, being PERILOUS.

Where your Saturn is found, there you are expected
to assume responsibility, to overlook coldness & to
work your hardest with patience and without thanks.
In the 1st, 2nd or 3rd House, he throws you on your
own early in life due to your father's misfortunes.
Saturn will be 6 houses after another whose persons
either throw their work on you or die early in life.

Where Jupiter brings plenty of whatever is shown
by the Sign and house he is in, Saturn is limiting.
Jupiter is expansive (and also expensive because he
gives out freely and generously). You are outgoing
and gregarious, conciliatory and charitable - where
Saturn is reticent, solitary and sternly just about
forgiving and forgetting. In this vein, Jupiter is
said to be for-giving and Saturn for-getting. But
no more loyal friend or teacher could be asked than
Saturn, the one-man-planet: Jupiter loves everybody
alike & is the preacher while Saturn is the priest:
Jupiter being merciful & requiring only repentance,
Saturn being just, exacting both penance & penalty.
These two conjunct are "penny-wise & pound-foolish".

URANUS

URANUS' symbol ♅ includes the letter H that begins the name of his discoverer Herschel, which was
originally the name for Uranus himself as listed in
the old ephemerides. Because he rules the house of
circumstances in life not in your control at birth,
the 11th that can lead you up to the Success-10th -
or down to the Failure-12th - he has the ability to
take you up or down in life according to the power
he exerts in your chart by his position and aspects.

By polarity with the Sign Leo he favors Leo people,
unaccountably giving them higher position than they
have been prepared for by training, rather than de-
mote them to the 12th, so Leo people seldom despair.

Uranus shows where you do the unexpected: if retrograde he is a repeater & so are you (all retrograde
planets go back and repeat), and since he rules all
lightning-like, spontaneous and unrehearsed actions
he represents instant response without equivocation
one way or the other. Where he is by house you are
destined to break ties and be free of domination or
unwholesome conditions: there you also will rebuild
on a better foundation, that being his reformation-
nature and intent. He is a non-conformist, a free
soul and a free thinker, radical, universally bent,
altruistic and exceedingly humane. He never does
things by halves; whatever he undertakes will be on
a grand or heroic scale and complete - though he be
crucified for it & receiving no thanks at the time.

Uranus will be 4 houses after another whose outcome
and future development will be unusual & frequently
surprising and unexpected. In any angular house
he leaves home as soon as possible, changes address
very often, suffers separation or a form of divorce,
appears in court, departs from the norm in whatever
the house rules, comes to public notice, & attracts
attention because of his appearance and his manner.
You either lose the father early or do not love him.

When in the Sign on the next-following house he has
a 12th-House tendency to disappoint your hopes-and-
wishes regarding the people & matters of that house
just as he upsets your well-being when in the 12th.
In the 11th, 3rd or 7th and also badly aspected, he
forms unwise attachments or unbonded relationships.

Uranus' keyword is "I KNOW" so that when he is well
placed by Sign and aspect (particularly to a planet
in or ruling the 1st House) he gives the answer almost before the question is asked. He possesses an
aptitude for the occult and innate mental awareness
of esoteric meanings, thus he is ruler of Astrology.

MARS

MARS' symbol ♂ is that of a shield-and-spear so
that he is the warrior planet showing where YOU are
equipped to fight for a cause. He is best situated
in the 11th House of particular circumstances where
you are sure of bettering conditions for yourself &
in general battling to achieve your hopes & wishes,
especially if your chart is afflicted. Wherever he
is by house, that is where you will have trouble in
life & where you must exert yourself to overcome it.
If in mutual reception (two planets in each other's
natural Sign) you have a talent for sidestepping or
getting out (or keeping out) of trouble and danger.

In any angular house he causes accidents, lawsuits,
arguments, many changes of address, obstacles to be
met, and the need to protect yourself. You tend to
go to extremes: overworking, scornful of setbacks &
dauntless in tackling any task; independent, enterprising, pioneering, trail-blazing, given to making
fresh starts and rash decisions. Because of rising
to any challenge you are easily drawn into debate &
sometimes disputes, being naturally excitable, but
grudges never last long unless he is fixed by Sign.

Mars is less rash & headstrong when in a succeedent
house, though just as independent and enterprising;
with more likelihood of shouldering burdens because
of marital finances, the care of children or due to
deaths in the circle, circumstances in life and the
need to overcome a tendency to spend extravagantly.
In any cadent house Mars provokes trouble with relatives, neighbors, in-laws, teachers or schoolmates
as well as employés, tenants & sometimes strangers.
He causes feverish illnesses, acute while they last
but soon over; accidents, hospitalization, & danger
of incarceration or seclusion in the 12th afflicted.
Mars and the Moon in any aspect will cause surgery.

NEPTUNE

NEPTUNE'S symbol Ψ is the trident of the god of
the sea, ruling that within us that is too deep for
us to fathom, because seen as through a veil darkly.
He represents everything mysterious; fogs and films,
shadows, sudden collapses, fainting & feinting, sub-
terfuge, subversion, treachery, defrauding & ambush.

As the higher octave of Venus, he rules the perfect ideal, the unattainable Utopia, unutterable or
inarticulate longings, the highest spirituality and
the lowest animalism, the unconscious mind and all
the ills that assail mental balance: chaotic thinking as well as sublimity; grotesque form purporting
to represent beauty; blind fascination & seduction.
Neptune can slay a person or a reputation or commit
suicide as well as anything else illegal or illicit
& yet be moral, immoral or amoral according to what
is shown by the arbiters of the chart (the strength
or weakness of the organic Sun & functioning Moon).

Neptunian veils, films and fogs cover reality in
a way at once deceptive and deceitful so that he is
capable of betraying himself and others, as well as
his country; of entering into nefarious schemes and
plots, aligning himself with mobs in mass hysteria,
of perpetrating big and little frauds, conniving to
swindle others of their rightful ownership, even of
their right to think for themselves because he will
enslave if he can (being natural ruler of the 12th-
of-enforced-servitude), thus the native himself can
become a slave to Neptunian drugs, alcohol, habits,
untruths and self-deception. He also rules alibis,
assumed names as an alias or pen-name or pet name.

Being an idealist, Neptune seeks to beautify the
prosaic or homely in life, therefore he rules paint,
cosmetics, veils, poetry, mirages, & romantic love.

MERCURY

MERCURY'S symbol ☿ represents the Winged Messenger, the angel of breath, who carries the Life Principle from the Giver of Life to animate all beings. He is the carrier & go-between, communicator of all sense perception, awareness of feeling & understanding or interpretation; our indispensable "answering service" in the body by which we respond physically to any initial outside stimulus. In the animal, he operates as instinct; in the child as intelligence, & in the adult as intellect - and inspiration which means a drawing to one's self of divinely-based and unplanned ideas that fire the imagination toward an extra-sensory perception leading to accomplishment.

This he does by the simple act of breathing in, the oxygen in the air thereby carrying the divine ether through the Mercury-ruled Gemini lungs to the bloodstream that maintains the whole body-intelligence & specifically that of the functioning of the brain & the mental image that is the foundation of Memory.

Mercury is the smallest of the celestial bodies and the general significator of a small child yet without him there would be no bond between the parents, which is to say the Spirit and the Mind; so that it is moreover written "A little child shall lead them" which especially refers astrologically to planetary knowledge which he transfers to the Aries brain, in which he coordinates physical-and-mental faculties.

Mercury and Jupiter rule the four cadent houses and their keywords explain our adult thought-processes: the Gemini-3rd, I THINK & the Virgo-6th, I ANALYZE: the Sagittarian-9th, I UNDERSTAND & the Pisces-12th I BELIEVE. Cadent houses end the four quadrants of the natal chart, so that the quadrant in which your Mercury was placed at birth gives your general key-

word describing your adult thought-processes; if in
mutual reception anywhere (two in each other's Sign)
show him also where he would thus appear in his own
Sign, still holding his same degree, revealing that
you possess an additional descriptive mind-keyword.

Mercury rules decisions, a 3rd-House attribute, and
being dual he rules the decisions that you make for
yourself according to the house he is in as well as
the decisions that you make for anyone and anything
ruled by the house he is 3 houses after; in angular
houses he makes decisions for the succeedent houses.
In succeedent houses, for the people and affairs of
the cadent houses; in cadent houses, for people and
affairs ruled by the angular houses. Thus you have
that responsibility according to his house-position
in your chart, and whenever he is aspected; whether
by a progressed or directional planet or a transit,
(which also applies to his mutual-reception place).
These points also show where you use your judgment.

Mercury in Cardinal Signs is more apt to do his own
thinking and initiate new ideas and new methods for
general usage; he is a pioneer; this also describes
him when in an angular house. In Fixed Signs he is
excellent at establishing ideas and methods already
begun by the Cardinal Signs, looking toward results
both practical and rewarding - which also describes
him when in a succeedent house. In Common Signs he
puts into circulation by the spoken or printed word
what the Cardinal Signs inaugurate and Fixed Signs
establish; this too describes him in cadent houses.

Now take Mercury in your chart and combine the reading for him according to his house-&-Sign position.
If cardinal-&-angular he pioneers something that he
himself inaugurated; if cardinal-&-succeedent he pioneers something started by another; if cardinal-&-
cadent he circulates something he himself started.

Mercury's elongation

By Mercury's elongation we mean his distance before or after the Sun which is never more than 28°,
so that only the conjunction, parallel and possible
orb of semisextile are attainable by regular aspect.

(Mercury in mutual reception anywhere may also
be read as though back in one of his own Signs
Gemini or Virgo where he may be in any regular
aspect to the Sun, revealing an additional and
otherwise-unseen Mercurial power in the chart)

However, it is not their aspects that concern us at
this point, but the elongation separated into three
equal divisions or DISTANCES corresponding to three
Signs that give important clues in reading Mercury.

In an over-all sense Aries rules the BRAIN which
registers all physical, mental & spiritual impulses
from whatever source as impressions. We have awareness of what goes on inside and outside of the body
through nerve responses by sympathetic extension of
emotion whether grounded on the physical, mental or
spiritual plane; and this awareness is in the MIND,
ruled by Gemini and changed into THOUGHT by Mercury.
He is the Intelligence resident in every body-cell,
responsive to call from whatever source, delivering
his de-coded message to the right brain-department.

Mercury the significator of logic & reasoning is
always relatively near the brilliant Sun so that we
all possess these mental attributes to a greater or
lesser degree of brilliance, evaluated by Mercury's
condition in the natal chart. By condition we mean
whether he rises before or after the Sun, is direct
or retrograde or intercepted or in mutual reception
as well as the type of Sign & house he is found in
and the nature of any planet between him & the Sun.

Mercury's three distances
0-9° 9-19° 19-28°

Mercury's 28-degree elongation divides into his
1st distance 0-9°, his 2nd 9-19° and his 3rd 19-28°
which reflect the vibrations of the three Air Signs
in which he has decanate-rulership. Their keywords
are Gemini, I THINK (because I use my mind); Libra,
I WEIGH (because I analyze my thoughts) & Aquarius,
I KNOW (because I arrive at a personal conclusion).
Without this logical procedure we could not express
Mercury's mental powers of intelligence & intellect.

Mercury within 0-9 degrees of the Sun, before or
after, works like a conjunction along Gemini lines,
giving an aptitude for logical reasoning from first
causes to an intelligent conclusion; he is coherent
in expressing himself, volatile & childlike in manner, desirous of learning, given to making gestures
or pouting; kinfolk & papers are active in his life.
In marriage the native may not fully appreciate the
good points of the first mate until after 10 years.

Mercury within 9-19 degrees of the Sun on either
side works like a sextile along Libra lines, giving
a judicial type of mind, fair and just, unemotional
and impersonal, generally a good judge of character
in choosing a mate; impressionable & susceptible to
persuasion; pure in mind, in speech and in motives.

Mercury within 19-28 degrees of the Sun operates
like a trine along Aquarian lines, denoting one who
thinks for himself and is broad-minded, universally
attuned toward human problems, diplomatic, tolerant
toward the frailties of others, charitable, unselfish and philosophical, capable of heroic decisions,
able to see both sides of a question and not argue,
but one whose opinion once reached is unchangeable.
He should guard against taking the easiest way out.

Mercury's condition in the chart

Considering the Sun as if on the Ascendant, show
Mercury by Sign & degree; if above the Ascendant he
is rising before the Sun; if below the Ascendant he
is rising after the Sun. In a Cardinal Sign, he is
self-initiating: that is, he does his own thinking,
has his own ideas, makes his own plans. In a Fixed
Sign he has a talent for establishing ideas & plans
initiated by others. In a Common (adaptable) Sign,
he adapts material already initiated or established
by others and presents it, or rather distributes it
wholesale so to say: puts it into wide circulation.

Mercury rising before the Sun

Rising before the Sun he looks before he leaps &
plans more carefully than otherwise; is self-taught
to a great extent and in the written or spoken word
may light the way for others because he carries the
torch of the Sun, about whom God said "Let there be
light" (enlightenment, intelligence and knowledge).
He tends to make his own way in life and gets ahead
despite circumstantial obstacles; to learn quickly,
to dispense with formality by disdaining the beaten
path and making his own small rules and regulations
and he remembers vividly the people and experiences
surrounding his early environment. Usually an avid
reader, his quest is mainly for facts & principles.

Mercury rising after the Sun

Rising after the Sun he is more serious and less
optimistic about what he is facing - being a little
in the dark - & often fearful of being left behind.
He can take a good education but is aware of a lack
in himself or innate inability to cope unaided with
what is expected of him but faithful to a trust and
quick to consider all well lost in the name of love.

Mercury direct

Mercury direct is so sure of himself that he has
fewer hurdles to jump in his forward dash towards a
goal, being quick on the draw as the saying goes, &
prone to accept another's challenge without reading
the small print; he is the easily-persuaded planet,
susceptible to error & often subject to correction.
Nonetheless he is a shrewd and clever adversary and
best to have on your side. If he or his dispositor
is in an angular house at birth, the native is sure
to make the headlines; several times if in a Common
Sign because they are repeaters & he rules encores.

Direct, he is never backward about being forward
therefore he usually "arrives" earlier in life than
when retrograde; makes overtures or introduces himself easily & is readily accepted without question,
thus more likely to achieve more than one marriage.

Mercury retrograde

Mercury retrograde is a closer observer of facts
and details, having more power of concentration because by "turning away" he shuts out whatever tends
to distract his attention. He is held back in life
or frustrated in earlier years but has the patience
to bide his time, hold his tongue discreetly & keep
his own counsel while gathering the knowledge he is
to use later, because the retrograde condition lies
waiting and there is always more to the person than
meets the eye. He has the capacity to go back, and
such a Mercury harbors no grudges, is eager to make
amends and therefore likely to be often imposed-on.

Mercury retrograde causes shyness and a retiring
disposition, not as ready as Mercury direct to make
public appearances unless in an angular house. His
fussiness makes him overly fastidious about details.

Mercury in mutual reception

Mercury and another planet in each other's Sign,
as Mercury in Capricorn and Saturn in Virgo, are in
a mutual relationship called mutual reception which
gives exchange status by agreement. It allows each
planet a secondary reading as though it returned to
its own Sign in another house where it has a second
opportunity to express itself or a chance to change
occupation or get out of what it got into unwisely.
It also offers the native a place of refuge, safety
or sanctuary at a time of some disaster in his life.

If the mutual reception involves a malefic planet that thereby can be read in an angular house the
person can easily get out of what he got into - but
not to his advantage because the malefic will be in
his own First House or square or opposition to him.
The chart on page 38 shows Jupiter & Uranus in mutual reception allowing Uranus to be read also in the
7th where marriage is gotten out of but by divorce.

Mercury intercepted

Interceptions mean interference, frustration due
to being held back or held down, personal aims held
in abeyance and if it is Mercury it is traceable to
relatives or someone represented by the house he is
in. In many ways it is similar to being retrograde.

Intervening planets

A planet between Mercury and the Sun affects the
mind accordingly: Saturn sobers it; Uranus frees it
from conventionality; Neptune bestows extra-sensory
perception; Mars kindles the imagination & develops
independence in thought & speech; Jupiter and Venus
give optimism, a cheerful outlook and peace of mind.
The Moon shows a sympathetic, emotional, moody mind.

Planetary Cycles & Years (see p. 212)

Of the 36 years contained in each cycle, certain
years are ruled by Mercury as listed here for those
years most likely to interest us from 1873 to 1979.
Those born in a Mercury year have Mercury prominent
in their charts, their lives & their personalities.

Cycle	Mercury Years
Mercury	1873, 1880, 1887, 1894, 1901, 1908
M a r s	1912, 1919, 1926, 1933, 1940,
M o o n	1951, 1958, 1965, 1972, 1979,

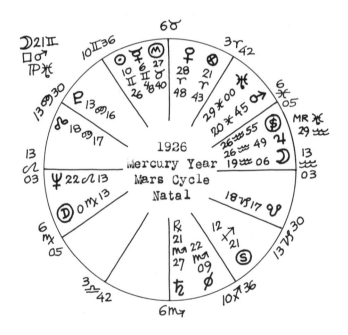

1926
Mercury Year
Mars Cycle
Natal

This is the natal chart of Marilyn Monroe, movie
actress born 6/1/1926, 9:37 a.m. LMT, 118W15, 34N04

The famous and beautiful actress Marilyn Monroe,
whose chart we present on the opposite page, was an
outstanding example of the prominence of Mercury in
the life of one born in a Mercury year with Mercury
by elongation in his own 1st (Gemini type) distance.

She was an intellectual type, given to much reading, valuing her books above all else, always learning as we would expect with Mercury leading the Sun
and carrying the torch of enlightenment. In the 1st
distance she was childlike, even naive in her dealings with others, trustful with Jupiter in the 7th,
idealistic with Neptune in the 1st trine Venus; and
maternally tolerant toward the frailties of others,
as shown by the Moon in Mercury's Aquarian distance.

Mercury rising before the Sun and in the career-
10th brought great success especially in the spoken
word (Gemini), and wealth by ruling the money-2nd &
conjunct the golden Sun, her Ascendant ruler. With
no planet in earth she was not materialistic at all
and beyond her books had few possessions - her home
being very plainly, even sparsely furnished as seen
by austere Saturn in the home-4th retrograde and in
square with the domestic-Moon and Jupiter-of-luxury.

Neptune in the 1st House trine Venus made her an
idealist in love, but this is not a grand trine and
thus her search for happiness always fell short because the trine "fell out" in the empty affectional
5th where her idealistic nature was not understood.
Even the benefic Jupiter in the marital 7th brought
no luck because by mutual reception with Uranus who
thereby operated in the 7th marriage meant divorce.

At age 36 the Part of Death 6 Libra was trine to
Mercury, and the Moon 21 Gemini squared Mars in the
8th, and she committed suicide.   (See pages 58-60)

* * * * *

VENUS

VENUS' symbol ♀ is that of a hand-mirror that -
like her face in it - reflects love-liness.   Where
Venus is placed by house, there do you love to be &
are most loved; the matters of that house are those
you love best.   Angular houses lean toward physical
and human attraction; succeedent, toward material &
financial attraction; cadent, toward intellectual &
abstract attraction.   Venus is just the reverse of
Mars (♀♂) being peace-loving, docile, obedient,
submissive, placid, gentle in speech, appreciative,
affectionate, mannerly and feminine in her approach
where he is bluntly masculine.   She loves comfort &
ease, harmony and security in life and environment.
Being the Lesser Benefic, she shows where you help,
encourage and benefit others -- and they you, also.

Venus is always in the remunerative 2nd House after
another house from which you will eventually profit.
She is always in the mental 3rd House after another
representing a person who considers you handsome or
beautiful as the gender may be, & who never forgets
you.   She is always in the end-of-the-matter 4th of
another house whose service, outcome, affairs, etc.
always prove satisfactory & most acceptable to you.

She is always kind & accommodating in any house but
in any cadent house she represents a woman having a
behind-the-scenes influence in the adjoining angle,
affecting for good or ill the career, marriage, etc.
Saturn in strong aspect to Venus cools the capacity
to demonstrate one's affectional nature; kissing is
avoided although it is otherwise a Venus attribute,
and the native generally feels unwanted by a parent.

Being a benefic, Venus in an angular house protects
the health, family life, marriage & all contractual
matters, & safeguards the reputation and occupation.

Venus' elongation

In the preceding section we devoted ourselves to
the elongation of Mercury (his solar distance, 28°)
and since Venus is the only other planet that stays
within a prescribed distance from the Sun (hers being 48°) we find her elongation very discernible in
the chart and thus in the native to whom it belongs.

(Like Mercury, Venus in mutual reception with
any other planet is given a secondary reading
as though back in one of her own Signs Taurus
or Libra from which she may be in any regular
aspect with the Sun, revealing an additional,
otherwise-unseen Venusian power in the chart)

Venus is the significator of appreciation of anything beautiful especially pertaining to human self-
expression as in the fine arts such as painting and
sculpture, architecture, interior decoration, music,
dancing & the theater. She rules the principle of
peace, persuasion, forgiveness, reconciliation, the
velvet touch, amiability, social contacts, charity,
balance and proportion in the artistic distribution
of the parts to the whole, and cohesive properties;
anything that binds cooperatively as in a marriage.

The closer Venus is to the Sun the more of these
attributes are apparent in the person who therefore
achieves better balance in life, maintains friendly
relationships, carries no grudges, has more possessions and greater security and enjoys better health
and more charm & magnetism in manner and appearance.

Venus in the same Sign with the Sun will always
have more friends among women in a man's chart, but
attract more friends among men in a woman's chart.

Venus' three distances
0-16°   16-36°   32-48°

Venus' 48-degree solar distance divides into her
1st distance 0-16°, her 2nd 16-32° & her 3rd 32-48°
which reflect the earthy vibration of Taurus, Virgo
and Capricorn. Their keywords are Taurus I HAVE by
right of possession, Virgo I ANALYZE & APPRAISE the
value of inherent worth, and Capricorn I UTILIZE as
in balancing the use-of-beauty & the beauty-of-use.
They also reflect 2nd, 6th & 10th HOUSE vibrations.

Venus within 0-16° before or after the Sun works
like a conjunction along Taurus lines, making for a
possessive & sometimes jealous tendency in marriage
(which is Venus' main forte: she "marries" whatever
should be joined together harmoniously, artistical-
ly and also cohesively so that "the twain are one").
This Taurus I HAVE distance reflects 2nd House security, assuring the native more possessions & freedom from want in life than are otherwise warranted.

She brings great gain and many friends according
to the house she is in at birth, but less if she is
retrograde or held back by interception. She is so
obedient by nature, being exalted in the meek Sign,
Pisces, that when retrograde she is often apt to be
over-obedient, to bend too far backwards in efforts
to be overly obliging & to want peace at any price.
A malefic between Venus & the Sun in this area will
lessen her attributes of generosity & friendliness.

Venus within 16-32° of the Sun on either side is
like a sextile, giving great opportunity to rise in
life by exercising the Virgo talent for appraisal &
discrimination in which the native operates for his
own best interests, this being the self-nourishment
Virgo-&-6th-House attribute. He values recognition
in life & possesses the self-application to earn it.

Venus as far from the Sun as 32-48° reflects the
Capricorn vibration of specialization along serious
occupational 10th-House lines, taking over the management of (and responsibility for) the matters and
persons ruled by the house she is in. She provides
for their present gain & future security, establishing something there that also enhances his position.

The Capricorn vibration has the thrifty, shrewd,
forward-looking characteristics of Saturn who saves
by denying himself; wastes no shred of anything and
stores up knowledge as well as money or possessions
for expected future utilization by someone he loves
(or protects the future interests of those for whom
he works). The native may know insecurity in youth
and independence in maturity but he generally shows
more regard for others' interests than for his own,
his life-long habits of thrift being hard to break.

Venus, like Jupiter, is a benefic in any life no
matter how afflicted the person's chart or fate may
be because a benefic is a saving grace making allow-
ances for human weaknesses or mistakes, compulsions
or aspirations-to-succeed at any cost. She grants
some recompense or deliverance in times of trouble.

Those born in the following cycles & under Venus
year-rulership have outstanding Venusian attributes
of appreciation of security & relief in emergencies.

Cycles	Venus Years					
V e n u s	1801,	1808,	1815,	1822,	1829,	1836
Jupiter	1840,	1847,	1854,	1861,	1868,	
Mercury	1879,	1886,	1893,	1900,	1907,	
M a r s	1911,	1918,	1925,	1932,	1939,	
M o o n	1950,	1957,	1964,	1971,	1978,	
S u n	1982,	1989,	1996,	2003,	2010,	
Saturn:	2021,	2028,	2035,	2042,	2049,	

3:48:20 a.m. LMT Jan. 12, 1893, Long 12E05, Lat 47N

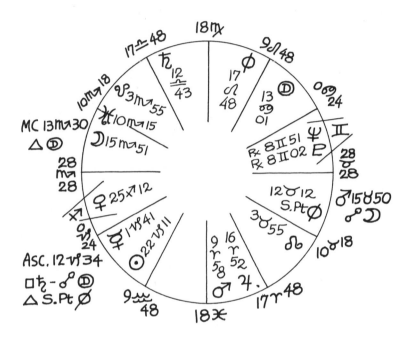

This is the natal chart for Hermann Goering, the Nazi held responsible with others for atrocities in obeying flagrantly monstrous commands to order vast numbers of helpless human beings to their deaths in Germany's many concentration camps in World War II.

He was sentenced to be hanged on Oct. 16th, 1946 as shown by a malefic in the execution-10th afflicting his own ruler Mars; but on the eve of execution he committed suicide by poison, escaping hanging by Venus in the 1st House & his ruler conjunct Jupiter.

Hermann Goering was born in 1893 which is listed
as a year ruled by Venus, a benefic, so that he was
due to rise in life & be protected from harm at the
hands of others. Venus in his 1st House and ruling
his 11th of hopes-and-wishes gave him everything he
wanted in pleasures, plaudits (and decorations too,
because in the caparisoned parade-Sign Sagittarius)
and we note Mercury-of-medals in his possession-2nd
coming from the Government-10th House that he rules
and he was as bemedalled as any in the Third Reich.
Venus in the title-and-regalia Leo decanate brought
him high military rank & an array of grand uniforms
which is again confirmed by his ruler Mars conjunct
Jupiter-the-magnificent in the showy Leo decanate.

But loving-kindness and mercy were not in him because Venus exactly semisquare Uranus is a non-conformist who pays no attention to noblesse oblige in
looking out for his own interests first when she is
in the First House. And in her 2nd distance 16-32°
from the Sun she has the cool detachment of the Virgo nutritive selectivity in appraising the value &
extracting the profit for himself.   Her semisquare
to Uranus on the obedient-12th thus inclined him to
servility-for-a-purpose in obeying those higher up.

That was his self-undoing. In every chart there
is an explanation for one's mistakes if we but look
for the reason, especially in some subtle or hidden
clue. Here, the ruler of his birth year, Venus, is
our source of revelation according to her strongest
aspect, her semisquare to Uranus, so that he is the
key to Goering's ineluctable fate whose pattern was
established at the precise moment of his conception.

How do we know this? By the rules for pre-natal
astrology activated when the natal Moon is conjunct
either Neptune or Uranus. Her Sign-and-degree were
on the horizon in the charts for conception and all

the pre-natal monthly lunar returns, 15:51 Scorpio,
and since Uranus hardly changes in a year's time he
was on the horizon for the entire gestation period,
a malefic afflicting the developing embryo: particularly involving his reasoning powers, since Uranus
rules his 3rd House where thought and logic reside.
Thus his year-ruler Venus and the Moon both pointed
to Uranus and the pre-natal Ascendant and afflicted
Goering's future thought-pattern thereby; unfortunately because in the 12th of illogical servility, &
the more noteworthy because born in a Mercury cycle.

For poisoning we look to Lilith & the 6th House:
for self-poisoning (self-assassination, or suicide)
we look to the Moon or a malefic in the 12th House.
Lilith's Solstice Point in the 6th is in bad aspect
to the midpoint between Uranus & the Moon-ruler-8th
(death) in the suicide-12th, and quincunx Saturn in
the execution-10th, making him his own executioner;
and by poison, because Lilith's effect registers in
the death-8th, according to the #14 Theory (p. 197)
Thus his year-ruler being benefic delivered him out
of the hands of the hangman into his own for death.

His progressions at death show great emphasis on
suicide. His ruler Mars 15:50 Taurus in bad aspect
to the Moon ruler-death-8th in the suicide-12th was
personally applying to death by his own hand - made
easy to do by progressed Sun trine Moon in the 12th.
The Ascendant 12:34 Capricorn was in evil aspect to
Saturn in the execution-10th & to the Part of Death
in the 8th. The 10th in 13 Scorpio was exactly conjunct the Uranus-Moon midpoint in the suicide-12th,
& his year-ruler Venus 2 Pisces semisquared Jupiter
in-&-ruling the grave-4th so she could not save him.

By age-arc 53° the Part of Death 6 Virgo exactly
sesquared the Sun, and Venus 18 Aquarius was in bad
aspect to Lilith-of-poisoning and to his Fate-10th.

* * * * *

PLUTO

PLUTO'S symbol ♇ combines the first two letters
of his name (some say it is the initials of his discoverer Percival Lowell). He is the farthest-out of
the planets and is by nature distant and shy, also,
preferring isolation.   Contrarily enough, he rules
groups, but among them he takes a silent & detached
position, similar to that of an orchestra leader or
the head of the Federal Bureau of Investigation, or
the silent partner holding some important position.

He is associated also with the underworld and those
considered beyond the pale socially, assuming their
characteristics as a disguise, taking on their manner and vulgarity of speech and frequently given to
swearing under his breath.   In the 1st House of an
afflicted chart the person puts his worst foot forward when confused.   He has a watchful look in his
wary eyes, walks aimlessly but is ready to take off.

Wherever Pluto is found by house, there may be complications to expect in life & difficulties to sur-
mount alone.   Because of his readiness to abandon a
situation that investigation deems hopeless, he may
be considered unreliable under pressure, a runaway;
an important person absent at an outstanding event.

Pluto is a disappointing factor as regards the matters and persons of the house he is in although the
native can easily detach himself & thus ignore them.
When in the Sign on the next-following house he has
an unsatisfactory and disappointing effect on whatever that next house represents to the native - but
again he can render himself insensible so to speak,
ignoring the conditions there.   The native is given
to shyness, nervousness, self-consciousness and con-
fusion in the presence of the people represented by
the house Pluto is in, and avoids them particularly.

♈ ♈ ♈ ♈ ♈

THE MANY WAYS OF RETROGRADE PLANETS

To be retrograde means to be philosophically conditioned to being held back, to accept limitation &
take the long way around, to adjust to the indirect
approach in working harder for what one wants, & to
value the opportunity for intensive advancement giv-
en by being set apart from others "on one's own" as
it were. Striving against odds always develops the
muscular power on all three human planes: physical,
mental and spiritual. Do not downgrade the retrograde planets in your chart: rather, recognize them
as blessings in disguise bestowing fine attributes.

If retrograde at birth these attributes are lifelong, becoming still more ingrained as the years go
by, and are traceable to the force of circumstances
in youth. When in the first three houses or in any
angular house, they operate earlier in life and are
more easily discernible in the native in childhood,
affording a valuable clue to his future life-work.

Retrograde planets work more on the inner plane &
signify greater opportunity for growth & attainment
through tapping inner resources, thereby disclosing
that we have them to tap: we were born with them, &
they mean "there is more to us than meets the eye".
There is always a time lapse before reaching a goal
but always an aptitude for self-application to work
that eventually justifies the native's every effort,
being the "evidence of things not seen" (Heb. 11:1).
Lessons, ideas, skills of early youth are stored in
the background, unseen as of future value until the
design at maturity asserts itself, & they fall into
place as inner resources. The retrograde condition
always gives power to go back and regain something.

Keywords for a retrograde planet

The keywords for the retrograde condition use its first two letters RE, taken both positively & negatively according to the planet's good or bad side. Saturn-the-Limiter, for example, is negatively limited and restricted in early youth according to the house he is in: but as Saturn-the-Undertaker (which works more ways than one) he has positive equipment to turn within and research his inner resources for whatever he wants to undertake in life.   The worse his aspect to the Ascendant or First House the more he resists being turned aside from his aim in life.

A planet in zodiacal aspect to another planet (or the Ascendant) simultaneously aspects it by mundane or house position, also.   These may both be good or one may be good, the other bad.   Energetic Mars may be in the 3rd House in good sextile by house to the 1st House but square the Ascendant "in the zodiac".

If in good aspect to the Ascendant but bad aspect by house, he is required to succeed without outside help, reorganizing his methods and retrenching when necessary to reduce the power of reversals.   He has to reconcile himself to meeting resistance in life.

If in bad aspect to the Ascendant but good aspect by house, he reflects dynamic power in exerting himself toward a goal and receives outside assistance, encouragement and appreciation from those described by the house he is in, because such houses by trine or sextile (3rd, 5th, 9th, 11th) befriend the First.

A retrograde planet is resented by or repulsed by the people of the house it is in, and refused early recognition, but the retrograde direction gives the power to go back and try, try again: the person has the ability to reverse & reconcile all differences.

Any planet, more especially a retrograde malefic,
square the Ascendant zodiacally or square the First
House by mundane aspect (house position, which will
simply be by being in the 10th or 4th House) indicates a person who never retreats, one who cannot be
turned from his chosen path: though held in durance
vile, he bides his time and reassembles his forces.
If opposition the Ascendant, much will be withheld
from him by open enemies, persons of either the 7th
or 6th House.   If conjunct the Ascendant from the
12th House side, enemies are hidden or unrecognized
as such: and if conjunct the Ascendant from the 1st
House side, the native is denied some environmental
security in youth and bears a physical birth result.

Always note the house in which the planet's power
acts and reacts by Wynn's #14 Theory in subtracting
the number of the house the planet is in from 14 to
find the number of the house reacting. A retrograde
planet in the 3rd is retiring by nature so that the
native sees little of his relatives, neighbors, etc.
which is thus true of his friends & club-members of
the 11th House (14 - 3 = 11).   Planets in the 1st &
7th Houses remain unchanged, as the student can see.

In any house including the #14 position, a retrograde planet is a repeater. What the native did in
the past he will do again; returning to a former interest or location, repeating a former action and a
retrenchment because of circumstances, rebuilding &
improving by reforming, according to the people and
the matters represented by the houses of the planet.

A retrograde planet recovers in time, both philosophically and materially: the person recoups whatever he may have lost, especially in succeedent and
angular houses; in cadent houses he readjusts well,
and also likes to go back mentally or to reminisce,
to recall old times: such houses rule recollection.

A retrograde planet standing alone will dominate, rebuke and be personally responsible for the people and affairs of the house it is in. It fends for itself and others there as from a detached position & thus draws attention to the native as well as great respect. He is the one-and-only to the persons of that house, while to the native himself his one-and-only is the person of the house ruled by the planet.

On the negative side, a planet retrograde denotes a person of the house it is in as resented, refused inclusion in the circle, repulsed and disinherited, put out of the house or family & forever renounced. Yet the positive side makes the native retain touch with the absentee, nonetheless, as a responsibility.

A planet retrograde draws back because of shyness and resists publicity and personal appearances when standing alone in the Sign or house. In a group of planets, one retrograde is in a detached position & uncomfortable, getting away as quickly as possible.

To be retrograde is to regress within so that the native learns by in-tuition, research & revelation; he is considered recondite, a word meaning mysterious, remotely profound & given to secret knowledge. Such persons are possessed of inner reasoning power and such planets register strongly in their future.

More is required of a person with more retrograde planets than one; he registers ethically because he recognizes this moral obligation early in life, and has ability to renounce his personal desires in the name of duty, conscience & honor, reacting to outer persuasion and responding always to noblesse oblige.

Retrograde planets well-placed by Sign are not so conditioned to remembering injury by others, nor to be guilty of recrimination or re-hashing of ills.

If the retrograde planet is Mercury, Saturn, Mars
or Venus the native is likely to be a perfectionist
bent on returning to his work to better it somehow.
Mercury writes & rewrites the same thing endlessly;
Saturn researches diligently & always relentlessly,
while Mars regains lost ground thru extreme effort.
Venus repaints the house and moves the furnishings,
changes trimmings and decorates the food & herself,
always with the readjustment idea of beautification.

A lunation falling on a planet retrograde whether
at birth or by progression will cause a reaction at
that time and a repercussion in two weeks and again
but less noticeably when returning in another month.

An eclipse conjunct or opposition a planet retrograde at birth or by progression excites a reaction
at that time & a repercussion in three months; also
when it is opposition or conjunct its first contact.

A progressed planet aspecting a retrograde planet
(and more noticeably the Midheaven or Ascendant doing it) will stir up affairs over a long period and
reactivate old matters, the effect depending on the
strength or weakness of the aspect. When coming to
the midpoint between two planets natally retrograde
the effect is noteworthy and both good & bad result
will transpire, as by gain along with renunciation.

A minor cusp (2d, 3d, 5th, 6th & their opposites)
conjunct a planet retrograde in these houses causes
a repetition of something ruled by the house as the
3d conjunct a retrograde planet in the 3d causing a
trip related to a previous trip, or a return visit.
In the 8th, a death in the circle similar to a previous death, or surgery following previous surgery.
In the 6th, recurrent symptoms of the same illness,
or replacement of a pet - & so on around the chart.

★ ★ ★ ★ ★

THE IMPORTANCE OF DECLINATION

The Sun's 18-degree-wide path through the zodiac
is called the ecliptic because eclipses occur there.
The Celestial Equator is the earth's equator extended out into space but because of the tipping of the
earth's poles from vertical the Celestial Equator &
ecliptic are not parallel; thus the ecliptic curves
above and below the Celestial Equator or "declines"
away from touching it, giving the word declination,
or distance north & south of the Celestial Equator.
Its greatest variance is 23°26'38.75" on each side,
astronomically termed the Obliquity of the Ecliptic.

♈----T-h-e---C-e-l-e-s-t-i-a-l---E-q-u-a-t-o-r-----

Planets in the first six Signs are above the Celestial Equator in North Declination because that is
the Northern Hemisphere marked by the Northern Sign
Cancer. From that point the Sun declines, crossing
the equator to reach the Southern Sign Capricorn in
the Southern Hemisphere, where the last 6 Signs are
below the equator & therefore in South Declination.

The Solstices and Equinoxes

Declination is given in the ephemeris along with
longitude. Note that the Sun's declination 23N27 &
23S27 is the same as the obliquity of the ecliptic,
which he sets when in 0-Cancer & 0-Capricorn: these
mark the turning-point Summer and Winter Solstices.
Declination therefore begins on the equator and is
0N00 in 0-Aries and 0S00 in 0-Libra, and these mark
the equal-days-&-nights Spring and Autumn Equinoxes.

To calculate declination

Declination may be increasing (leaving 0-degrees) decreasing (retrograding to 0-degrees), or changing in direction (crossing 0-degrees to either N or S). See Mercury's declination in the ephemeris for this.

Always set down the GMT-line in detail as exampled:

If the Declination is increasing on the GMT-date, work it as a direct planet .. D

P.m. GMT means plus: A.m. GMT means minus

```
9:25 pm GMT Jan 5 (⊬ 5th)
                  4063 C.L.
Jan 6, 19S15 D
 "  5,  19S10
        0:05 = 2.4594 log
           ⊬  .4063 C.L.
⊬ 5th,  0:02 = 2.8657 log
        19S12 = Decl. Moon
```

If the Declination is decreasing on the GMT-date, work it as though retrograde. R

The opposite of what the GMT says to do.

```
6:45 pm GMT Dec 8 (⊬ 8th)
                  5509 C.L.

Dec 9 -15N11 R
 "  8  17N22
        2:11 = 1.0411 log
           ⊬  .5509 C.L.
- 8th,  0:37 = 1.5920 log
        16N45 = Decl. Moon
```

If it is changing on the GMT-date, ADD the 2 places together. Subtract the small motion from the place on the GMT-date: if too great, subtract the place from the motion but mark it the opposite direction..........

```
8:00 am GMT Feb 4 (- 4th)
                  4771 C.L.
Feb 4,  1N06 C
 "  3, ⊬3S20
        4:26 =  .7335 log
           ⊬  .4771 C.L.
- 4th,  1:29 = 1.2106 log
SWITCH -1N06 = GMT date N
        0S23 = Decl. Moon
```

The parallel of declination

The value of declination in astrology is that it
gives us the parallel, a most powerful and magnetic
aspect that always attracts & has the total holding
power of a conjunction if the declination-direction
is the same for both planets.   If one is in North
declination and the other South, they are attracted
by the magnetism of the parallel but since they are
opposite in declination-direction they lack holding
power, like an opposition that separates eventually.

What you have at birth in conjunction or conjunction-type parallel you will keep forever.
What you have at birth in opposition or oppos-
ition-type parallel you will eventually lose.

The two planets may be in either good or bad aspect otherwise. It is the parallel that emphasizes
their power and duration in life.   What you get by
square comes with effort; what you get by trine and
sextile comes easily.   In either case, you keep it
if the declination is the same in direction. If it
differs in direction you achieve it but you lose it.

Keep a list of parallels for any kind of chart -
natal, horary, mundane or ingress, or any important
event such as marriage, partnership agreement, separation or divorce, declaration of war or peace, or
filing a legal document, etc. - marking the declination North or South as the case may be so that the
lasting or separating effect is easily ascertained.

Where appropriate, the chart should include the
Part of Fortune, Marriage, Partnership, Sickness-&-
Upset Conditions, Death, etc., (p. 61) & these also
should have their declinations listed. The declination of any of these is simply that of the Sun in
the ephemeris when he is in the same Sign & degree.

The seemingly-minor Part of Sickness for example
includes Upset-Conditions-in-General, and in varied
charts has major significance: in personal illness,
financial & domestic upset, distress in company and
institutional or national conditions, and whether a
local or national disaster, epidemic, crime wave or
other unfortunate development, etc. will last long.

For a personal reading we repeat the natal chart
given on p. 38 for the beautiful and famous but ill-
fated actress Marilyn Monroe. We shall confine our
reading to the parallels that account for her great
success in life and her equally great unhappiness,
her several divorces, and her suicide after winning
fame and fortune. We are indebted to the astrologer
Blanca Holmes for the personally-secured birth data.

9:37 a.m. LMT June 1, 1926, 118W15, 34N03

(S)	22S19
Sun	21N55
Merc	21N15
(M)	19S04
Lil	18S15
Moon	17S00
ASC:	16N37
Sat	15S50
Nept	14N29
M.C.	13N33
Jup	13S21
($)	12S38
(D)	11N16
Ven	8N55
Fort	8N31
Mars	5S44
Uran	1S05

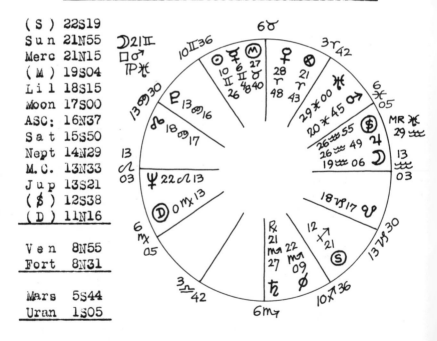

Allowing 1° orb, we note the parallels of declination emphasizing unique continuity in 13 out of 17
listed, denoting a person with a LADDER to climb in
life and thus sure to rise; especially with the Sun
at the very top, thus signifying a brilliant career.
When you find many parallels in continuity at birth
you find a person who will come before the public &
attract attention whether favorable or unfavorable.

Her early environment was extremely unstable due
to Neptune in the 1st House being square Saturn who
in the home-4th is conjunct malefic Lilith the dark
moon of the earth: she is the satellite whose power
is directed mainly against the mother.   Marilyn's
mother was unfortunate in life, unable to provide a
home or support her child, and this is confirmed by
the mother-Moon square Lilith & Saturn in the 4th &
opposition the orphanage planet Neptune in the 1st,
and the child was reared among strangers & orphans.

Neptune in the 1st House made her an idealist, &
the trine to Venus gave her a hauntingly wistful or
appealing type of beauty emphasized by the parallel
to Saturn who in a Water Sign is extremely magnetic.
Neptune is also parallel Jupiter the smiling planet,
and she had a lovely smile. But both parallels are
of the opposition type, Jupiter being South declination, Neptune North.   She was very volatile, able
to feel joyously happy one moment and sad the next,
Neptune attracting a response he could not maintain.

Neptune's parallel to Saturn in the 4th made her
idealize home life; to Jupiter in the 7th, marriage
was the ideal state for her. The parallel attracted
several marriages & homes but the declination-dist-
ance was opposite in each instance and there was no
lasting foundation, no holding power to cement them.
Jupiter and the Moon in the 7th sextile Venus & the
Part of Fortune in the legalizing-9th allow several

marriages but shortened by Saturn's square and also
unfortunate by their square to the Part of Marriage
in the 10th & ill-starred by conjunction to the so-
called Weeping Sisters (Pleiades), so that marriage
would always be ill-starred & would end in weeping.
Aquarius on the 1st or 7th has much to do with divorce ending either this marriage or a previous one.
Neptune or Uranus angular, even by mutual reception
as Uranus 29 Aquarius is here, separate or divorce.

Leo on the Ascendant & the ruler Sun in the 10th
of ambition-and-success sextile the rising degree &
conjunct the 11th of circumstances in life gave her
great success by her own efforts, having to do with
speech and acting as ruled by Gemini and Leo. Neptune in the 1st House and in Leo gives natural acting ability, the trine to Venus-ruler-10th assuring
ease in reaching stardom by good Fortune because of
Neptune's simultaneous trine to the Part of Fortune
and his conjunction-type parallel to the Midheaven,
so her success & fame will live on after her death.

The Sun-ruler-1st conjunct and parallel Mercury,
ruler money-2nd, & both of them sextile the Ascendant, granted self-earned wealth. The natural ruler
of the 2nd, Venus, conjunct the Part of Fortune and
sextile Jupiter-of-wealth brought her great riches.

The worst afflictions are the parallel-square in
Fixed Signs between Saturn-the-Reaper-conjunct-Lil-
ith-of-suicide and the ruler of the death-8th, Nep-
tune-of-suicide (by sleeping-pills or anything that
induces a comatose state): also the afflictive par-
allel-conjunction of the Part of Suicide (⚵) 26:55
Aquarius to Jupiter who co-rules the 8th of death.
Marilyn committed suicide on Aug. 5, 1962 by sleeping-pills as the Moon 21 Gemini sextiled Neptune in
the 1st, squared Mars in the 8th & by exact declination 1N05 with Uranus' paralleled him in the 8th.

⚸ ⚸ ⚸ ⚸ ⚸

THE ARABIAN POINTS

The widely-used Arabian Points are more commonly called Parts (as the Part of Fortune, etc.) and are arithmetical degrees based on the natal Ascendant. They are directed by exact age-arc (p. 216 herein) to aspect natal positions, and they receive aspects from progressed planets & angles and from transits.

The Part of	Derivation	
Brethren, Kinfolk ..	= Asc ∤ Jup - Sat	
Catastrophe	Uran - Sun	
Commerce, Business..	Mars - Sun	
Contentment, Peace..	Ven - Sun	
Daughters	Ven - Moon	
Death, Disaster	8th - Moon	(D)
Discord, Inharmony..	= Asc ∤ Jup - Mars	
Faith, Belief, Trust	Merc - Moon	
Father, Advancement.	Sun - Sat	
Fortune, Substance..	Moon - Sun	
Increase, Benefits..	Jup - Sun	
Inheritance, Legacy.	Moon - Sat	
Intelligence, Skill.	= Asc ∤ Mars - Merc	
Love, Entertainment	Ven - Sun	
Marriage, Partners..	7th - Ven	(M)
Mother, Family	Jup - Ven	
Peril, Danger	ruler 8th - Sat	(P)
Play, Sports	Ven - Mars	
Servants, Service ..	Moon - Merc	
Sickness, Upset Cond	Mars - Sat	(S)
Sons	= Asc ∤ Jup - Moon	
Spirit, Soul	Sun - Moon	
Suicide	8th - Nept	($)
Surgery, Cutting ...	Sat - Mars	(C)
Tragedy, Fatality ..	Sat - Sun	
Treachery, Fraud ...	Nept - Sun	(T)
Waste, Extravagance.	= Asc ∤ Jup - Mars	

The Part of Legalizing (L)
The Part of Weddings (W)

This writer adds the Part of Legalizing (L) that
is based on the 9th House ruling ritual ceremonials
that formalize and legalize the native's 7th-House
contractual affairs such as agreements & especially
weddings (W) legalizing otherwise common-law unions.
The formula is the 9th plus the 3rd and minus Venus.

The Part of Bereavement (B)

This writer's Part of Bereavement (B) is derived
from the bereavement-12th cusp plus its ruler, then
minus Neptune (planet of widowhood) but it includes
bereavement of any person of the house it occupies,
as well as widowing of the native whose chart it is.
Vindemiatrix 8:41 Libra is the "Star of Widowhood".

The Part of Assassination (A)

This writer's Part of Assassination (A) is based
on the Ascendant plus the ruler of the 12th & minus
Neptune. In the ingress chart on p. 149 forecasting
the assassination of President Kennedy (A) 2:51 Gemini fell in the 5th (death-8th for the presidential
10th House) & squared the Part of Death in the 8th.
In his natal chart, p. 151, it was 7:57 Leo sextile
the Sun in the 8th (and square Mars in the ingress).

Their Solstice Points

The Solstice Points of the Arabian Parts ATTRACT
ATTENTION to their importance by progression and to
their own nature. They always mark a TURNING POINT
in the life of the native, and will have to do with
something ruled by the planet. In the natal chart
on the opposite page for President F. D. Roosevelt,
whose health was afflicted in adult years by polio,

7:45:36 p.m. LMT January 30th, 1882 ..... 74W 41N45

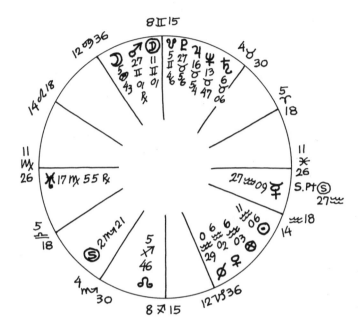

the Part of Sickness (S) 2 Scorpio in the 2nd House
(the oncoming Future) exactly semisquared Uranus of
crippling in the 1st House (the Present) signifying
a future illness that would start as acute (Mars) &
become chronic (Saturn) due to the nature of these
two planets that make up the formula for (S).   Its
Solstice Point (S) 27 Aquarius "attracts attention"
to Mercury who rules the physical Ascendant & is in
the 6th-of-illness exactly square Pluto the malefic
who compounds complication upon complication of any
sort.   The saving grace lay in the mutual reception
between Uranus & Mercury (each in the other's Sign)
so that Uranus can be read as incurable in the 6th
but Mercury in the 1st can be read as able to hold
his own in life -- even to register as a President.

5:23:19 a.m. LMT June 12th, 1896 .... 76W41 39N

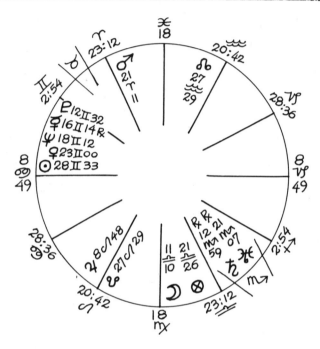

This is the natal chart for the Duchess of Windsor,
who at age 31 unexpectedly inherited $75,000 from a
relative. Her age-arc 30:33 brought FORTUNA to the
conjunction of Uranus-of-windfalls and moved Uranus
to 21 Sagittarius trine Mars (gain through a death).

In June 1967 she was at last officially accepted by
Queen Elizabeth as a member of the royal family, 30
years after her marriage to the abdicated King of
England. Her Part of Marriage & Part of Advancement
both 24 Aquarius at birth now by age-arc 69:59 were
conjunct their joint Solstice Point 5 Scorpio marking a TURNING POINT in her life, a rise by progress
having to do with marriage. Jupiter 18:47 Libra now
trined Neptune, each co-ruling the recognition-10th.

☿ ☿ ☿ ☿ ☿

Keywords for Sign decanates by houses

The late Ben Gary, astrologer, revived the ancient noun keywords for planets in Sign-decanates according to the houses occupied. For greater clarity we prefer the adjective "faithful" for the 3rd-House-&-2nd-decanate rather than "one of fidelity" & so on:

1st House
1st decan, active,busy
2nd "   high-minded
3rd "   articulate

7th House
1st decan, tactful & kind
2nd "   independent
3rd "   well-balanced

2nd House
1st decan, determined
2nd "   endeavoring
3rd "   capable,apt

8th House
1st decan, resourceful
2nd "   responsible
3rd "   prevailing

3rd House
1st decan, intuitive
2nd "   faithful
3rd "   logical

9th House
1st decan, devotional
2nd "   pioneering
3rd "   academic

4th House
1st decan, sympathetic
2nd "   sensitive
3rd "   questioning

10th House
1st decan, organizing
2nd "   establishing
3rd "   eliminating

5th House
1st decan, commanding
2nd "   reforming
3rd "   ambitious

11th House
1st decan, original
2nd "   inspired
3rd "   altruistic

6th House
1st decan, achieving
2nd "   experienced
3rd "   renouncing

12th House
1st decan, realistic
2nd "   unselfish
3rd "   merciful

☆ ☆ ☆ ☆ ☆

WHEN THE BIRTH TIME IS APPROXIMATE

When the time of birth is given as approximate it
tells us that the Sun is related to a certain time-
cusp, as: near the 6th around 8:00 p.m., <u>Local Mean
Time</u>. The date of birth tells us the Sign & degree
he is in to be put with him on that cusp in a trial
wheel as a starting-point. In the Table of Houses
& under the birth latitude this cusp gives the Midheaven and remaining cusps; enter the planets also,
to choose the one to aspect in rectifying the time.

Either the PROGRESSED Midheaven or Ascendant will
be the key according to the age-arc & planet in use
at the time of the first event of major importance,
and it leads us to finding the true time of birth.
We will present two examples illustrating the point.

The first major event in life

It is ordinarily very easy to rectify the approximate time of birth by the first major death in the
family (because it is the first break in the circle
that directly affects the native) but if an earlier
misfortune occurs, such as loss of a parent through
divorce or other cause, or an accident that renders
the native permanently injured or incapable of taking care of himself, such events are equally usable.

The importance of the Midheaven

The correct time of birth gives the correct Midheaven and Ascendant which will register under progression to time the major events in life. We want
to find the True Calculated S.T. for that Midheaven
and we do it through the Progressed Midheaven's S.T.

The PROGRESSED Midheaven's Sign & S.T.

The age in years tells the distance in degrees between the Midheaven or Ascendant and a planet it is
to aspect.   That planet's degree is the degree that
the PROGRESSED Midheaven or Ascendant must reach at
aspect (it will reveal its Sign).   For a Midheaven
aspect we take that Sign, Degree and Progressed S.T.
as on the 10th cusp in the Table of Houses. For an
Ascendant aspect, its Sign & Degree on the 1st cusp
gives its Progressed Midheaven's Sign, Degree & S.T.
It is always the PROGRESSED Midheaven we work from.

The number of days after birth denotes the age in
years & gives the Progressed Date. For a p.m. birth
take the Sidereal Time on that date and also on the
birth date.   For an a.m. birth, take the Sidereal
Time for the day before the Progressed Date & also
the day before the birth date. The difference between the two you use is the increase to subtract
from the S.T. for the PROGRESSED Midheaven, giving
the Approximate Calc. S.T., only a few minutes off.

The True Local Mean Time at birth

Using the Local Mean Time represented by the cusp
the Sun is near, work the Trial Calculated Sidereal
Time: the difference between this & the Approximate
Calculated S.T. just found gives minutes of difference to add to the Local Mean Time you used, & this
gives the corrected Local Mean Time for the birth.
For a p.m. birth it is also the interval-since-noon
but for an a.m. birth add 12 hours for the interval.
With this corrected Local Mean Time Interval, work
the chart as usual for the True Calc. Sidereal Time,
correcting the minutes in the Approximate Calc. S.T.

The LMT plus the EGMT for W. Longit. places gives
the GMT. For E. Longit. places, subtract the EGMT.

Aspecting by the Midheaven

This is the case of a woman who gave her father's
death in Sept. 1961 as the first major death in her
family, occurring when she was age 43. She was born
around 3:00:00 p.m. PDST July 17, 1918, 123W52 47N.
That would put the Sun 24 Cancer near the 9th cusp,
Virgo on the Midheaven, & Mars 12 Libra in the 11th
(the death-8th after the father-4th).   To conjunct
Mars the Prog. M.C. must be 12 Libra (12:44:08 S.T.
in the Table of Houses). The Prog. Date, Aug. 29th.

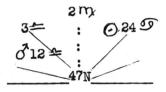

Check the rules on p. 67 as you study this example:

```
        10:27:32 S.T. Prog. Date Aug. 29, 1918
      -  7:38:00 S.T. p.m. birth July 17, 1918
         2:49:32 S.T. increase 43 days (years)
  from 12:44:08 S.T. MC 12 Libra to conj Mars
         9:54:36 Approximate Calculated S. T. *

         2:00:00 p.m. LMT for Sun near the 9th
         0:20 10-second correction Interval
         1:22 10-second corr. EGMT  8:15:28
    ✝    7:38:00 S.T. at birth July 17th, 1918
         9:39:42 Trial Calculated Sidereal T.

  from  9:54:36 Approximate Calculated Sid. T.
         0:14:54 Difference to add to 2:00 p.m.
    ✝    2:00:00 p.m. LMT for Sun near the 9th
         2:14:54 p.m. LMT 17th TRUE Birth Time
                 gives 9:54:42 True Calc. S.T. *
    ✝    8:15:28 EGMT for birthplace 123:52 W.
        10:30:22 p.m. GMT 17th = 3590 Const/L.
```

At age 43 the Progressed Midheaven conjoined Mars
and confirmed the father's death by sesquaring Uranus ruling-and-in the father-4th house.   That it was
death was confirmed by progressed Part of Death (D)
26 Cancer exactly quincunx (death angle) to Uranus.

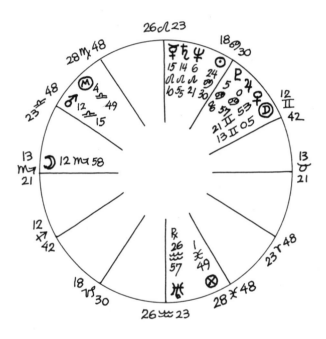

Once having determined the correct hour of birth,
all other important events in the life are expected
to register.   This woman married on Oct. 29th, 1944
cementing instead of breaking the circle so that it
would take second place to a death in rectification.
The Progressed Midheaven 24 Virgo sextiled the Sun
in the ritual-9th; the Progressed Moon & Mars in 27
Libra trined Uranus, and her age-arc 26:00 directed
the Part of Marriage (M) 0:49 Scorpio trine Jupiter.

The exactitude of (M) & (D) prove the cusps correct.

Aspecting by the Ascendant

   This man is the husband of our first example, and
they were born 1 day apart: he on July 18, 1918, at
122W54 48N at around 3:00 a.m. PST, which would put
the Sun 25 Cancer near the 2nd cusp, with Pisces on
the mother-10th & her ruler Neptune also in the 2nd.

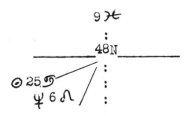

For his mother's death at his age 32, the Ascendant
should be 6 Leo conjunct Neptune with M.C. 18 Aries.
The Prog. Date Aug. 19th but use the previous dates
Aug. 18th & July 17th, because it is an a.m. birth.

```
        9:44:10 S.T. Prog. Date August 18th
     -  7:38:00 S.T. July 17th (a.m. birth)
        2:06:10 S.T. increase for 32 years
from    1:06:10 S.T. Prog. M.C. in 18 Aries
       23:00:13 Approximate Calculated S.T.  *

       15:00:00 a.m. LMT interval (+ 12 hrs
        2:30 10-sec. correction Interval
        1:21 10-sec. corr. EGMT  8:09:20
     +  7:38:00 S.T. previous noon, July 17
       22:41:51 Trial Calculated Sid. Time

from 23:00:13 Approximate Calculated S.T.
      0:18:22 Diff. to add to 3:00:00 a.m.
     + 3:00:00 a.m. LMT for Sun at the 2nd
       3:18:22 a.m. LMT 18th TRUE Birth T.
                gives 23:00:16 True Calc ST  *
     + 8:11:36 EGMT for birthplace 122W54
      11:29:58 a.m. GMT 18th = 1.6532 C.L.
```

At his mother's death in March 1951 the Prog. M.C.
18 Aries gave the Prog. Ascendant 6 Leo exactly conjunct Neptune and exactly semisquare Part of Death,
21 Virgo (ruled by Mercury who turned retrograde in
his year 1950/1951 denoting a year involving death)
confirmed by the Progressed Moon conjunct the 8th.

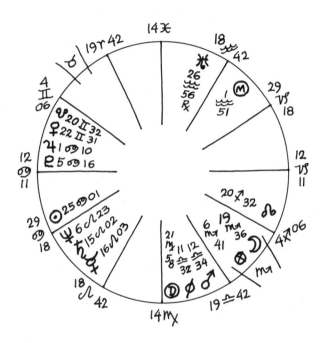

That the death would be sudden & unexpected is revealed by unpredictable-Uranus receiving the square
of the progressed 11th (death-8th for family-4th) &
opposition of progressed Sun ruling her illness-6th.
Transiting Uranus turned direct to exactly conjunct
Pluto-co-ruler her death-8th (this 5th). The Sun &
her co-ruler Jupiter both 22 Pisces opposition Part
Death squared Venus ruling her 8th. The Moon ruler
her 4th (this 1st) in 26 Taurus was square Uranus.

☿ ☿ ☿ ☿ ☿

THE WAY OF

A PROGRESSED CHART

PROGRESSIONS and REGRESSIONS

A person's birth chart is his pattern in life to unfold its promise as time goes on and developments materialize, both good & bad, for him to live thru. From his first breath, he & his chart make progress together, as shown by the new positions his planets reach and the aspects they make to natal positions.

At the rate of a day for a year in his ephemeris the planets move forward by progression & backward by regression in the pre-natal period but they both register AFTER birth. For a birth on June 12, 1940 mark June 13th as 1941 progressed, and June 11th as 1941 regressed, and so on for 90 days after as well as 90 days before birth for a lifetime of 90 years. The year in which both progressed & regressed planets are simultaneously active will prove important.

A badly afflicted chart is still fortified somewhere to meet & recover from the impact of the blow. The trouble is, we don't always see it until afterwards, on regaining equilibrium & realizing that we met and handled the situation & got by successfully, and the progressed chart itself discloses the clues.

Zodiacal plus Mundane aspects

The secret lies in knowing how to offset the two aspect-formations we always have simultaneously but do not ordinarily combine as we should. One is the zodiacal aspect involving Signs and degrees and the other is the mundane aspect involving relationships by house-to-house. The two are always in action at the same time & should be taken into active account together because the one can often offset the other.

The effect of the impact

Anything happening in your life also happens in
your chart & causes the houses to stir accordingly.
The activating planet sets up a chain reaction that
in an angular house arouses ALL the angular houses:
in a succeedent or cadent house it arouses all the
succeedent or cadent houses & it will be by conjunction, square & opposition whether or not they have
planets in them (in which case they react with more
or less impact - but they react). If an activating
planet aspects the Ascendant or only the Ascendant,
which from angular, succeedent or cadent houses may
be any aspect at all, the native will be personally
involved in whatever happens: the stronger the aspect, the more significant his personal involvement.

Angular houses have IMMEDIATE impact. Trouble
brought by an afflictive activating planet there is
sure to register somewhat before or after the time
it designates: 6:00 a.m. & p.m. or noon & midnight,
which is a hint to those expecting something amiss.
For example, if you know that transiting Mars is to
conjunct, square or oppose a malefic in any angular
house in your chart, avoid dangerous occupations or
places (of accident) around the major hours of day.
A malefic in the 4th at birth "localizes" danger in
the vicinity of home & on the home grounds, & so on.

Succeedent houses have DELAYED impact. Trouble
brought by an afflictive activating planet there is
likely to establish something wrong that takes root
before you know it & you recognize its urgency only
when outward symptoms appear, which is usually near
3:00/4:00 a.m. or p.m., or 11:00/12:00 a.m. or p.m.

Cadent houses have CONTINGENT impact. That is,
they depend on something else to bring to light the
trouble revealed by an afflictive activating planet

there that is being temporarily suppressed awaiting
further developments or authorization & enough time
in which to make known the news about what happened.
There is a time lapse for cadent houses so that the
full impact is delayed & the native finds out about
what took place, good or bad, much later; generally
in a roundabout way or through others or by chance.
It frequently happens that the native receives news
about 1:00/2:00 a.m. or p.m., 7:00/8:00 a.m. or p.m.

The effect of the aspect

If the activating planet's aspect to a planet by
Sign-&-degree is the SAME as the aspect between the
houses they occupy, the zodiacal-and-mundane aspect
is the same and the effect is not changed. A trine
or sextile is then more fortunate and brings a time
of ease & gain but a square, quincunx or opposition
is then more unfortunate, bringing trouble or loss.
But if an activating planet's aspect to a planet by
Sign-&-degree DIFFERS from their house-relationship
the impact also differs and the effect is changed.

For example, a planet in the 4th square by Sign-
&-degree to a planet in the 1st will endanger real-
estate holdings, domestic affairs & family members,
etc., because the 4th House rules all these and the
1st House rules the native's personal ties & interest there, while the danger-by-square is both zodiacal & mundane. Squaring the Ascendant alone would
work the same way. But if the zodiacal aspect were
good, the mundane square would be appeased to great
extent in meeting the situation -- sometimes by the
expenditure of money to meet foreclosure or struct-
ural damage, or care for the family in some illness.

On the other hand, suppose the activating planet
were in the 1st House squaring a planet in the 4th:
the native himself would upset 4th-House matters by

selling out, breaking home ties, saddening the family or disrupting their schedule. But if the zodiacal aspect were good, the mundane square would result in gain by selling out or leaving home because
of personal advancement even though the family were
saddened thereby: the new schedule would be better.

Accompanying aspects

The principal activating aspect is a conjunction
or opposition from a progressed or transiting planet to a natal or progressed planet or angular cusp:
or falling on an angular cusp and squaring a planet
either progressed or directed by age-arc; or square
an angular cusp from the conjunction or opposition
of a natal, progressed or directed planet or point,
as the Part of Sickness, Surgery, Peril, Death, etc.

In making such a principal aspect the activating
planet may also make accompanying aspects elsewhere
in the chart at the same time, giving us additional
clues in a very helpful way in time of real trouble.

For instance, a square from the unfortunate 12th
House to a planet in the 3rd House is both zodiacal
and mundane, bringing belated news by cadent houses
of possible hospitalization or incarceration of one
of the persons ruled by the 3rd (relative, neighbor
or correspondent) but at the same time it may throw
a trine to the 8th of curative-surgery or a release
by payment of a fine, tax or alimony so that "all's
well that ends well" would be the tenor of the news.

If however the principal aspect was good but the
accompanying aspect was bad we would expect a favorable opportunity for gain that would occasion labor
or self-denial or extra cost before it materialized.
Not a time of trouble: we just "go to some trouble".

The TYPE of aspect

The square, semisquare & sesquare

These are PHYSICAL aspects in which the native's reaction in time of trouble either makes or breaks. He goes to extremes of effort, spends too much time or energy or money of his own volition, running the danger of causing resentment or alienation or exile. There is always some loss attached according to the houses involved and only a good accompanying aspect or a mutual reception can mitigate the severity and see the native home safe. At such a time he should bend every effort, count the cost and speak softly.

The sextile & semisextile

These are MENTAL aspects, each involving common-sense recognition of a prevailing situation or condition, especially as viewed from the standpoint of a disinterested third person able to accept reality. Such an activating planet's aspect is usually good, bringing a time of available opportunities in life; all the better if the accompanying aspects are also good to denote gain: if bad, expect some difficulty. You should acknowledge & evaluate the current state of affairs at such a time & not go off the deep end if the ever-so-rosy opportunity also has drawbacks.

The trine

The trine is a BIRTHRIGHT aspect granting ease & success in accomplishing what the activating planet signifies; you possess the talent, the right or the chance now to gain, even if it is only an accompanying aspect - as a possible inheritance at a time of trouble or death.   If the trine involves Jupiter, Venus, the Moon or Uranus-of-windfalls or the ruler of the 2nd, 8th, 5th or 11th (money) gain is sure.

The quincunx

The quincunx is a REORGANIZATION aspect based on
the distance from the First House to the organizing
Sixth and from the reorganizing Eighth to the First,
so that distress, illness or loss by death frequently characterizes its impact. Whatever occurs under
a progressed or major-transit quincunx from angular
houses upsets the status quo in life so that things
are on a different basis thereafter; never the same.

The conjunction & opposition

The conjunction & opposition are RELATED aspects
forever aware of the parallel of declination within
themselves so that the effect of such an activating
planet's aspect has significance now and forever in
the life whether the relationship continues or not.
The conjunction is generally good - the opposition,
bad - depending on whether a malefic is involved or
if the accompanying aspect favors a malefic or not.
In time of trouble, accept the situation and see it
philosophically as inevitable and out of your hands
because it may bring someone into your life against
your wishes or take away someone you dearly love -
each under circumstances out of your control. Mars,
Saturn or Uranus malefically aspected always denote
danger of an accident or the passing of a relative.

The parallel

The parallel is a most magnetic ATTRACTING power.
Two planets may be in any aspect at birth or by progression and also parallel at the same time. If in
declination they are both north or both south it is
a mutual attraction that endures and what is gained
is held forever; but if in opposite directions (one
north, the other south) the attraction lessens, the
hold weakens, and loss or separation is inevitable.

Mutual reception by Sign or House

In a certain particular instance, the impact can be turned about, reversing the effect by mutual aid. This is by Zodiacal Mutual Reception if the activating planet & the one it aspects are in each other's natural Sign OR by Mundane Mutual Reception if each rules the Sign on the house the other planet is in. It gives exchange status that enables them to reach an amicable agreement that is mutually beneficial, either for working together or getting out of whatever they got into - & meanwhile there is much less apprehension on both sides from the very beginning.

In times of trouble, always look to see if there is either a Zodiacal or Mundane mutual reception to get you safely out. A zodiacal mutual reception at birth protects you from any threat throughout life; if one of them is a malefic you have a charmed life. A mutual reception by progression is like a transit of Jupiter that protects for the transit's duration.

The part you play

The most direct action on your own accord comes from planets square, semisquare or sesquare the Ascendant or a planet in the 1st House, arousing you. A strong conjunction falling in your First House is also a personal incentive, usually bringing changes. The quincunx or "Finger of God" aspect is generally operative after some frustrating condition or someone over you moves out of your way so you are free.

The opposition is non-cooperative and forces you to work against odds, difficulties or some jealousy. Trines and sextiles, semisextiles & parallels grant desirable results with help from relatives, friends and strangers. If you have both good & bad aspects operating simultaneously you are repaid for losses.

Which way to turn

The nearest source of help or comfort to turn to will come from the house that is sextile to the 1st House if it contains a planet or if its ruler is in the 1st House or in good aspect to the ruler of the Ascendant or to a planet in the First House itself. With planets in the 11th or 3rd you always have the aid of friends, relatives or neighbors when needed.

The next-nearest source is the house that trines the 1st House if it contains a planet or if its ruler is in the 1st or in good aspect to the ruler of the Ascendant or to a planet in the 1st House. With planets in the 5th or 9th you always have what help you ask from children, in-laws or strangers, though some distance and consequent wait must be expected.

Help sometimes comes from a house that is square the 1st House if it contains a planet well-aspected to the Ascendant, its ruler or a planet in the 1st, although it may come grudgingly & entail repayment. These are the mother-and-Government-10th and father-&-family-4th; such a planet there promises some aid, but the mundane square to the 1st makes you earn it unless it is Jupiter or Venus, the Moon or Fortuna.

If the chart shows malefics angular you will act in your own behalf, easily or with effort according to their aspect to the Ascendant. If succeedent, you must act to establish whatever is ruled by that house. If cadent, you should act - by yourself or with the assistance of others, according to whether they aspect the Ascendant or not. But in any case, let the zodiacal-and-mundane positions disclose the best course to take, & then take it voluntarily and in that way establish your pattern as it should be.

* * * * *

THE OBLIQUE ASCENDANT IN PROGRESSIONS

To be oblique is to be slanted, a word also used nowadays to describe certain political opinions and "double-entendre" remarks having a subtle or hidden meaning, but when used in astrology it refers to an ascendant accompanying the Directed Midheaven whose presence reveals a subtle or otherwise-hidden force that when in aspect involves the native personally.

Adding the age-arc for any year to the Midheaven at birth gives the Directed Midheaven, used here to be located in a Table of Houses in order to extract its ascendant for the birth latitude; this we enter outside the wheel, and observe that it is "slanted" rather than parallel the horizon, so it is oblique.

Nothing could be simpler than this to figure and by the same token nothing could be simpler in finding many personally-important years ahead; agreeing that any ascendant must always be in aspect one way or another when personal affairs are being involved whether it be the natal ascendant or the progressed or directed or oblique ascendant. Oncoming aspects promise action, but unless one of the ascendants is included - or planets in the 1st House itself - the native is only indirectly affected by what happens to another person or matter or thing in his circle.

Since any ascendant has to do with latitude that is itself a parallel, the parallel aspect formed by the Oblique Ascendant is of primary influence - the more so when by conjunction - and specifically when conjunct the 2nd cusp, its first major "slant" away from the Ascendant. In aspects that include a parallel always name it first as: parallel-opposition. To be parallel means to be within one degree of being the same in declination (which is listed in the

ephemeris along with the planets' longitude) therefore we always list the natal declinations with the
chart for easy reference. Have an ephemeris at hand
so that the declination of the Oblique Ascendant is
readily found as it progresses, & it is simply that
of the Sun when he is in that same Sign-and-degree.
List also the declination of Fortuna, etc. this way.

The house of the immediate future

Where the 1st House rules the immediate present,
as at birth, and the 12th House rules the immediate
past preceding birth, the 2nd House rules the immediate future: the first intimation of the approaching personal trend in life that discloses one's inherent fitness for a particular interest to be followed as a career or vocation in the future.   This
is the special office of the Oblique Ascendant, and
where is the person who would not like to have this
information long in advance?   We need to know when
the Oblique Ascendant will conjunct the 2nd cusp so
as to know the age when it happens & thus the year;
and we want to know, too, what matters are ruled by
the house where we find the planet ruling that 2nd.
That is the house in which the native's main talent
is to register, and if the ruler of the 2nd is well
aspected to the natal Ascendant, the native's goals
will be more easily attained.   But if in bad aspect
(square, sesquare, quincunx, opposition) there will
be obstacles, delays, setbacks or denials to expect.

On the opposite page we present former-President
Harry S. Truman's natal chart set for 4:14 p.m. LMT
May 8th, 1884, Lamar, Mo., 94:15 West, 37:30 North.
The list of parallels shows by its arrangement that
he had a ladder to climb in life but his Ascendant-
ruler Venus is at the top, disclosing that he would
reach the top of the ladder in time and probably by
his own efforts, Venus standing alone in the house.

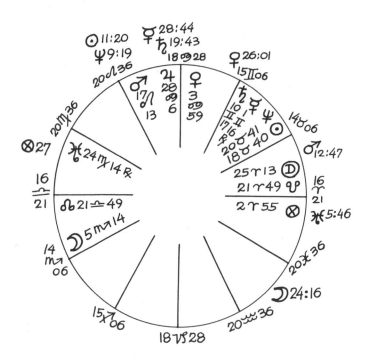

VENUS –	26N48	
Mercury	21N44	
Jupiter	21N09	
Saturn –	20N34	
Pluto –	20N31	
Marriage	20N22	
Peril –	17N39	
Mars – –	17N31	
Sun – –	17N24	
Neptune	16N18	
Moon – –	12S21	
Death –	9N40	
Uranus –	3N00	

Planets in the 1st House describe one personally active in furthering the matters of the houses they rule. If there at birth, it is a lifelong ambition; if there by progression or direction, it is an active interest for the duration of their stay.   In this chart, the Moon in the 1st reveals lifelong interest in a career because she rules this career-10th; trine Venus ruler of the Ascendant, he would certainly gain whatever he went after and moreover would never lose interest because of the Moon's fixity by Sign. The homeland Sign Cancer on the M.C. has to do with the Government; Jupiter there grants a high position of authority & a professional title.

The year of the event

To find the unknown year when the immediate future begins is just the reverse of finding the known
year. We will example both ways now for easy grasp
of the simple method, as for Mr. Truman. His career
began on March 30, 1918, when he was sent to France
as Captain in the American Expeditionary Forces during World War I.   From this first rung, he climbed
the ladder as Judge, Congressman, Senator and Vice-
President thence to President of the United States.

When the event year is known

Change the age to arc (see p. 216) and add it to
the natal midheaven to find the Directed Midheaven,
which gives the Oblique Ascendant whose declination
we also show to see any parallel-aspect it may make.

```
              3 18:28 Natal Midheaven
          ⊬  1 03:20 arc 33y 9m 22d (1918) CAPTAIN
Dir/M.C. Leo (4)21:48 = O/A 14 Scorpio, Decl. 16S10
                     Parallel-conjunct Future-2nd
```

When the event-year is not known

The Oblique Ascendant moves forward to make many
aspects, its progressed Sign-&-degree being the basis of our figuring.   Perhaps its most significant
aspect is its conjunction to the Future-2nd cusp so
this Sign-&-degree 14 Scorpio must be that of both.
In the Table of Houses under Latitude 37 this gives
the Directed Midheaven 21 Leo, set down as 4 21:00.
We need not use the natal Midheaven's minutes here.

```
2nd )
O/A ) 14 Scorpio (Lat. 37)  = Dir/MC 21 Leo or 4 21
                            − Nat/MC 18 Can or 3 18
O/A will conjunct the Future-2nd at age 33 = 1 03
```

The 2nd-of-Ownership shows what you possessed at birth, what you brought over with you: your TALENT, which in ancient times was the name of a Hebrew denomination of money (also ruled by the 2nd), valued up to $2,000, which is again the number of the 2nd. What you will do with your Talent and where it will be spent best is shown by the house (the department of life) where the ruler of your 2nd cusp is found. For Mr. Truman, Mars rules his 2nd & is in the 10th denoting a talent for government work & a political career: his sextile to the 1st gave the opportunity. In his onward career the Obl/Asc was mostly in good aspect to Jupiter elevated in the 10th granting him honor, recognition, title and a steady rise in life.

```
                  3 18:28 Natal Midheaven
              ⚹   1 07:27 arc 38-y (1922) ....... JUDGE
Dir/M.C. Leo (4)25:55 = O/A 17 Scorpio, Decl. 17S02
                          Parallel-sq. Mars, ruler 2nd


                  3 18:28 Natal Midheaven
              ⚹   1 21:00 arc 51-y (1935)...CONGRESSMAN
Dir/M.C. Vir (5) 9:28 = O/A 27 Scorpio, Decl. 19S38
                          Parallel-Saturn trine-Jupiter


                  3 18:28 Natal Midheaven
              ⚹   1 25:12 arc 56-y (1940) ..... SENATOR
Dir/M.C. Vir (5)13:40 = O/A 1:07 Sagit, Decl. 20S24
                          Par Jupiter, Mercury & Saturn


                  3 18:28 Natal Midheaven         VICE-
              ⚹   1 29:09 arc 60-y (1944) ... PRESIDENT
Dir/M.C. Vir (5)17:37 = O/A 3:24 Sagit. Decl. 20S54
                          Par Jupiter and trine Fortuna


                  3 18:28 Natal Midheaven
              ⚹   2 01:00 arc 61-y (1945) ... PRESIDENT
Dir/M.C. Vir (5)19:28 = O/A 4:55 Sagit. Decl. 21S10
                          Par-Jupiter, Mercury, Saturn.
```

The planet ruling the 2nd cusp shows by decanate
the part of life when the talent would register: in
the 1st decanate (up to 10 degrees) it should be by
age 30; the 2nd decanate (between 10 & 20 degrees),
between ages 30 & 60; the 3rd decanate (20 to 30 degrees) between ages 60 & 90. With this in mind, if
the ruler of the Ascendant (self) is in the first 5
degrees you will disclose your talent in childhood;
and if between 5 and 10 degrees it will be in later
teens before age 30. If between 10 and 20 degrees,
it will be in your early thirties or mid-forties or
your late fifties according to the degree itself; &
if between 20 & 30 degrees, it will be in the early
sixties, mid-seventies or even in the late eighties.

Mr. Truman's Mars-ruler-2nd is in the 2nd decanate denoting age 30, 40 or 50; in 17 degrees denoting the late fifties for special attention which we
find marked his first major advancement as SENATOR.

The difference in degree between the planets and
the Arabian Parts (of Fortune, Sickness (S), Deaths
(D), Peril (P) & Marriage (M) for which see page 61
indicates the age at events reflecting their nature.
Such events must occur in the future thus involving
the Oblique Ascendant at the time. Add the age-arc
to the Natal Midheaven as usual to get the Directed
Midheaven that provides the Oblique Ascendant whose
aspects show what is being activated. For instance,
the Part of Sickness (S) 23 Sagittarius will travel
to 3 Capricorn in 10 more degrees (years: age 10) &
oppose Venus who rules the physical Ascendant: thus
at age 10 he was near death due to serious illness.

```
                3 18:28 Natal Midheaven
             ✠  0 09:51 arc 10-y (1894) .. DIPHTHERIA
Dir/M.C. Can (3)28:19 = O/A 24:38 Libra, Decl. 9S28
                       Par-Mercury in near-death 8th
                       PERIL 20 Scorp op-Neptune-8th
```

```
              3 18:28 Natal Midheaven
            ⊬ 0 29:34 arc 30-y (1914)  DEATH/FATHER
Dir/M.C. Leo (4)18:42 = O/A 11 Scorpio, Decl. 15S08
                        Par-Nept/8th, DEATH-tr-Uranus
                        quin. Saturn-ruler-4th in 8th
```

```
              3 18:28 Natal Midheaven
            ⊬ 1 04:30 arc 35-y (1919) ..... MARRIED
Dir/M.C. Leo (4)22:58 = O/A 15 Scorpio, Decl. 16S47
                        Par-Mars ruler of marital 7th
                        (M) 3 Vir sxt Venus-ruler-1st
```

```
              3 18:28 Natal Midheaven      ATTEMPTED
            ⊬ 2 05:03 arc 66-y (1950) ASSASSINATION
Dir/M.C. Vir (5)23:31 = O/A 7:57 Sagit. Decl. 21S40
                        Par-Mercury ruler 12th in 8th
                        PERIL 15 Capri., sq Ascendant
                        Age-arc Neptune 25 Can sq (D)
                        Protected by parallel-Jupiter
```

```
              3 18:28 Natal Midheaven      OPERATION
            ⊬ 2 09:00 arc 70-y (1954) APPENDICITIS
Dir/M.C. Vir (5)27:28 = O/A 11:00 Sagit. Dec. 22S11
                        Par-Mercury in 8th-of-surgery
```

Forecasting based on the age-arc

In progressing Mr. Truman's chart ahead for 1957
this writer wrote late in 1956 that the arc for age
73 would move Fortuna conjunct the 9th and hoped he
would be blessed with a grandchild as ruled by this
9th (being the children-5th after his children-5th).

```
              3 18:28 Natal Midheaven
            ⊬ 2 11:57 arc 73-y (1957)  BIRTH G'SON
Dir/M.C. Lib (6)00:25 = O/A 13:13 Sagit. Dec. 22S23
                        Par-Jupiter & Mercury-rul-9th
Born 6/4/1957           FORTUNA 14:52 Gemini conj-9th
                        * * * * *
```

T H E   W A N D E R E R   R E T U R N S

Planetary Cycles in Progressions

In times gone by, the ancients differentiated between stars that are apparently fixed in their places and those that move in their courses and have a
definite motion that is usually direct but is often
retrograde, & this sets them "wandering" on various
"planes". They were thereby called wandering stars
or planets and were observed to move in cycles & to
return full circle to any Sign-&-degree position at
birth but in periods of time that differed with the
planets, designating such-and-such a cyclic year in
the person's life equivalent to his age at the time.

What a planet promised at birth by its position &
aspects was activated at its cyclic return which is
quite different from its return by transit, the two
being usually at variance. A planet completes its
cycle without reference to its transiting position,
the latter being unequal due to stationary periods.

On the next page we list the cycle-ages for Jupiter's return every 12 years, Mars' every 19 years, &
Saturn's every 30 years, marking their conjunctions
to their place in the natal chart, which stimulates
them anew in a personal way. We also list the half-
cycle ages when these planets oppose themselves and
the person meets with some opposition or setback in
his dealings with someone else. The quarter-cycle
brings the planet to square itself so that the person goes to extremes in developing his birth-right,
especially in expressing himself in his chosen work.

Uranus' full cycle is 84 years, his half-cycle 42
years, his quarter-cycle 21 years. Neptune opposes
himself at age 84 & squares himself at 42. Pluto's
cycle at 268 years allows only his square at age 67.

Planetary Cycles

Planets	Age at Conjunction Full-Cycle	Age at Opposition Half-Cycle
Jupiter	12,24,36,48,60,72,84	6,18,30,42,54,66,78
Mars	19,38,57,65,95	10,29,48,66,85 .....
Saturn	30,60,90	15,45,75 ....
Uranus	84	42 ....
Neptune	168	84 ....

Planets	Age at Square Quarter-Cycle
Jupiter	3,15,27,39,51,63,75
Mars	5,24,43,63,81 .....
Saturn	8,37,68 ....
Uranus	21 ....
Neptune	42 ....
Pluto	67 ....

As might be expected, those years marking the arrival of more than one returning planet would prove
more momentous in the life. For example, at age 30
Saturn returns to himself full cycle as Jupiter returns to oppose himself - both of them close on the
heels of the departing half-cycle Mars, so that age
29/30 has more than ordinary significance for gains
& responsibility in the wake of an important action.

At age 42, Jupiter, Uranus and Neptune operate in
the same year and, being major planets, they denote
a development in the person's life of major importance to him in a personal way. At 84, both Jupiter
and Uranus conjunct themselves while Neptune & Mars
oppose themselves in a giving-&-taking combination.

Planets retrograde or stationary

The cycle-ages are climactic in a way, since they
bring to a climax what the planets were building up
to: more significant and far-reaching if the returning planet were retrograde or stationary at birth &
thus marked R or S which singled it out for special
attention through life as one MARKED for the future.
Retrograde planets give the native power to come to
logical decisions & also to effect reconciliations.

Fixed stars and critical degrees

Planets conjunct or opposition fixed stars either
benefic or malefic are also marked for unusual, out-
of-the-ordinary circumstances when returning to the
conjunction, opposition or square of their original
positions in the natal chart. And they often bring
matters to a head or climax at such full or partial
cycle-returns if they held a critical degree in the
natal chart. The critical degrees are based on the
Moon's travel, 13° per day: they are 0-13-26 of the
Cardinal Signs, 9-21 of the Fixed Signs and 4-17 of
the Common Signs & (like Mars) cause crises in life.

Planets in mutual reception

Two planets, each in the other's natural Sign, as
Jupiter in Leo and the Sun in Sagittarius, are in a
mutual relationship called mutual reception. It is
a blessing and a protection, giving exchange status
so that each planet may also be read as though back
in its own Sign, still keeping the same degree, and
enabling the native to gain an advantage through an
outside person or a change of location: and it also
allows the native to get out of what he got into if
he wishes -- but if retrograde he usually stays put.

As a general rule, the more eventful developments
in the life are timed by planets in angular houses,
(the 1st, 10th, 7th, 4th) especially the slow ones.
Charts of outstanding personalities or those either
famous or notorious are almost certain to have slow
planets in angles, as will be noted in the chart we
now present for England's George VI who was born at
3:10 a.m. LMT Dec. 14, 1895, 0-Longit, 52:32 N. Lat.

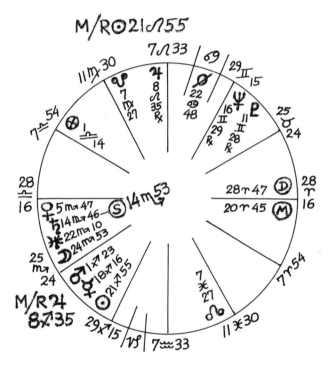

We shall give first place to Jupiter, seeing that
he meets the requirements for cyclic timing for all
the main events in the King's life and after death,
& we shall also mention Venus, his Ascendant-ruler.
For high position in life, Jupiter in the 10th is
in a commanding house, towering over the others and

MARKED R for special attention, conjunct the benefic fixed star S. Asellus that bestows riches & con-
fers executive authority (the more so in mutual reception with the Sun, ruler-10th and brilliant in a
Fire Sign and sextile the Ascendant from his mutual
reception position 21 Leo in the governmental-10th).

The mutual reception gives exchange status: here
it joins the ruler of the high-position 10th House,
the Sun, with Jupiter the ruler of the brother-3rd,
elevating him to kingship through the willing abdication in his favor of his brother, King Edward IX,
who renounced the throne in order to wed a commoner.

Moreover, Jupiter's secondary position in 8 Sagittarius in the money-and-substance-2nd conjunct Mars
in-and-ruling that house and sextile Fortuna in the
11th-of-Circumstances increased & enlarged his holdings and substance through fortunate circumstances.
All these Jupiterian benefits were his "birthright".

The return of Jupiter

Age 15 timed Jupiter's square at the death of the
grandfather (confirmed by Saturn's square also) and
the consequent coronation of the father; June, 1911.
Jupiter 5:25R Scorpio was transiting Venus in-&-rul-
ing the 1st House for his delayed (R) rise in life.

Age 27 timed Jupiter's quarter-cycle again at his
marriage in April, 1923 (the arc moving Mars-ruler-
marital-7th cusp to 28 Sagittarius trine that cusp).

Age 30 timed Jupiter's half-cycle at the birth in
April, 1926 of his daughter Elizabeth, destined for
the throne of England in her turn. Simultaneously,
Saturn returned to himself at the death in November
1925 of his grandmother Queen Alexandra, while Mars
still opposed his own natal position by half-cycle.

At age 41½ his coronation sealing his kingship in
May, 1937 involved the 42-year half-cycle of Jupiter & Uranus, and Neptune's quarter-cycle.   Jupiter
brought the benefit & Uranus the unexpected turn of
events, but it was the iridescent Neptune that gave
the glamorous tinge making the proceedings colorful.
Any aspect at all between Neptune and Mars at birth
gives a love of color and a colorful life, and this
King was born with Neptune & Mars in close parallel.

In May, 1950 at age 54 Jupiter's half-cycle timed
the recognition of the King's serious symptoms as a
cancerous lung condition, deemed probably terminal.
We direct the Arabian Points by age-arc, and age 54
took the Part of Sickness from 14 Scorpio (where it
meant a chronic condition by conjunction to Saturn)
to 8 Capricorn afflicting Jupiter by quincunx which
is an 8th-House termination-and-transition aspect.
The King became increasingly ill, & began preparing
Elizabeth for her oncoming accession to the throne.

Venus, ruler of the Ascendant

Age at Conjunction
Full - Cycle

8,16,24,32,40,48,56,64,72,80,88

Venus rules both the 1st House and the 8th in the
King's chart, marking his house of arrival on earth
by birth and also his departure from earth by death,
the two sides of the same door.   Venus is thus very
prominent in these eventualities in his present in-
carnation, both his birth & death receiving greater
publicity because she is angular & in the 1st House.

The death of the King's father on Jan. 20th, 1936
was timed at age 40 by Venus' 5th return to herself

in the personal 1st House, her square to Jupiter in
the 10th denoting a loss by death.   Deaths were all
around him in 1943/1944 at her 6th return at age 48
when the King was serving with his men at the Front
in World War II.   Her 7th return at age 56 brought
death to the King himself on Feb. 5, 1952 & also to
his mother, Queen Mary, on March 24, 1953 which was
a blessèd release for each because of the condition
of the malady that took them both. When Venus rules
the 8th the passing is gentle, usually during sleep
as it was for the King and his mother, when the arc
56:11 moved the solstice point of the Part of Death
from 1:13 Virgo to 27:24 Libra conjunct the Ascendant which is his beginning-1st and her ending-4th.

As ruler of the Ascendant and also a benefic, Venus' return at age 40 was a mixed blessing.   While
it put him in line for the throne that same year by
his brother's abdication the next December, she was
also square Jupiter in the 10th-of-honors but retrograde, denoting an advancement and honor this quiet,
home-loving man had never wanted, being retiring by
nature and not welcoming so prominent a position in
life with all the pomp and ceremony it would entail.
Those of us with Saturn in the First Quadrant never
dodge an issue or a responsibility, however, and he
accepted the call to serve his country, despite his
natural shyness & the frail condition of his health
due to the Part of Sickness conjunct chronic-Saturn.

The wheel keeps turning

The wheel keeps turning after the native has gone
on, and the King's two important significators, Venus & Jupiter, will return to themselves and square
each other at age 72/73 in 1967/1968 as they did at
age 40. In that period the Queen's pre-natal Saturn
changes direction & her progressed 10th squares Mercury, to time national changes, decisions and loss.

* * * * *

THE WAY OF

A HORARY CHART

A HORARY CHART

"Will Mr. R buy the carpet I advertised for sale?"

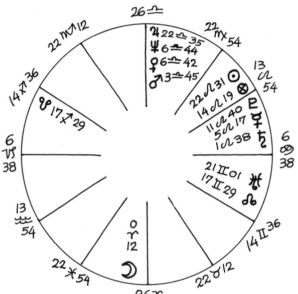

D△ħ·ⅠⅤ♀·♂♂·△♀·♂Ψ·ⅠⅤΨ·ⅠⅤ♂·♂♀·△Ⴒ·△⊗·ⅠⅤΨ·ⅠⅤ♂·ⅠⅤ♀·⚹⚸·♂♃·△⊙·ⅠⅤ♃
11:55 P.M. GMT AUG. 15TH   3:59 A.M. GMT AUG. 18TH

    The 1st House represents the inquirer-seller and
the 2nd his possession for sale (carpet).   The 7th
represents the one inquired about (Mr. R) the buyer
and the 8th is his money. The 4th denotes the end-
of-the-matter so far as the inquirer is concerned &
the Moon parallels its ruler Mars to signify a good
and favorable ending (which will not take long, because the Moon enters the 4th in only two more days
to make her final aspect, parallel Jupiter, revealing that the matter ends well & the answer is YES).

FOR BEGINNERS IN HORARY

From the writer's "Horary Astrology"

In astrology, to ask a question is to receive an answer - because there is always an answer to every question if we but knew it early enough to afford a chance to profit by it. This is that question-and-answer department of astrology called HORARY, where the chart is set for the time, date and place where a serious question is first "born" -- and only that first chart is dependable: never ask about the same question on that same matter more than the one time.

For beginners not yet acquainted with horary but appreciating what it can do for them in private and personal affairs they wish to keep that way, a very simple, basic set of rules will be all they require for a simple answer to an ordinary question such as the one on the opposite page. Apply these rules to this chart as we go along, then to one of your own. For terms new to you, refer to Terminology, p. 215.

Questions resolve themselves into action desired or anticipated, worried about or feared. Something will or will not happen: something is true or it is false: someone is safe or he is not: the illness is serious or merely transitory; the situation will remain as it is or a change is coming up - and so on. In questions calling for a yes-or-no answer we must reply definitely in the affirmative or negative; in any other kind of query we must also be definite in giving our opinion for or against whatever is asked about and we always do this mainly through the Moon.

We can always give a correct answer if the chart itself is correct. The first thing, therefore, is to be sure of the chart before we start to read it.

Is the chart correct?

If SATURN rules or is in the 7th House the chart
is incorrect somewhere, in figuring the cusps or in
figuring or placing the planets or Part of Fortune,
or in omitting something. Usually, we fail to note
the declination of the Part of Fortune --- which is
simply that of the Sun when he is in her Sign-&-de-
gree position, and which was omitted in this chart.
Check all the work and the chart accordingly at the
very outset. (In passing, it is moreover true that
this rule for Saturn also applies to natal charts.)

Is the Moon void of course?

If the Moon does not make any APPLYING aspect at
all from the Sign she is in she is void of course &
doing nothing, so there is no activity to expect in
the matter asked about.   An inactive Moon means an
inactive chart; nothing will happen but talk; there
is nothing to worry about or fear; no action can be
expected in the case, nobody is in peril or trouble,
etc., and this will be your answer to the question.
The chart proposes but the Moon disposes. This can
be reassuring & comforting to a sick or worried person because such a Moon says NOTHING TO WORRY ABOUT.

But if the Moon's declination is within a degree
of that of the Part of Fortune they are parallel, &
the Moon is not void of course: the answer is good.

Does the Moon aspect an Arabian Point?

Where you find the Arabian Point called Fortuna,
the Part of Fortune, something of that house is now
being improved and noticeably so if aspected by the
Moon. If by parallel, conjunction, trine or sextile the person is fortunate in asking and receiving
but if by square or opposition the improvement will

be neither complete nor lasting -- yet things could
have been worse, we say, and this is the time to be
philosophical about an improvement involving a loss
or a separation or denial in the matter asked about.

Significant Arabian Points

In questions about Marriage always show the Part
of Marriage (M), which is derived from the 1st cusp
plus the 7th cusp and then minus the place of Venus.
For a Wedding ceremony (W) or any Legalizing action
(L) the 9th plus the 3rd & then minus Venus' place.
For Sickness (S) the 1st plus acute-Mars then minus
chronic-Saturn.   For surgery or Cutting it is (C),
the 1st plus chronic-Saturn, then minus acute-Mars.
For danger or Peril (P) take the 1st plus the ruler
of the 8th, then minus Saturn.   (Thus, if Capricorn
is on the 8th, the Part of Peril will be exactly on
the Ascendant since we both add & subtract Saturn.)
For the Part of Death (D), the 1st plus the 8th and
then minus the Moon --- but it is never your death.

If a void-of-course Moon applies to such a Point
in a question it is related to it saves her from being void of course; and the nature of her aspect to
it, good or bad, affects the nature of your answer.

The Moon's condition

If the Moon is in a Sign ruled by a planet that
is now in Cancer they are in each other's home Sign;
a mutual arrangement that we call mutual reception.
It gives exchange status revealing that some change
or exchange or give-and-take by mutual agreement is
likely to be considered in the proceedings and also
that the inquirer can get out of what he gets into;
but if his ruler is retrograde he may decide not to
do so because of responsibility, duty or a penalty.

If the Moon is in an intercepted Sign it denotes
interference in the matter; a blocked course & some
message, person or thing intercepted in transit, or
the matter asked about is held up for awhile, since
interceptions hold matters in abeyance. But if the
Moon is also in mutual reception somewhere she will
find a way out of the difficulty when she is ready.

If the Moon is in the 6th House itself or is six
houses after the one bearing her Sign Cancer she is
in distress; something is not working right and she
will require more time to adjust it or find a cure.
When the Moon is in the 5th or 9th House, something
will affect the final outcome as by a petering-out,
renunciation or lessening of interest; these houses
having their end-of-the-matter-4th in the unfortunate 8th and 12th but less so if benefics are there.
The 4th House tells how the matter asked about will
end: the Moon there brings some changes in the end.

If the Moon is directly between two malefics, no
matter how far apart they may be in different Signs
or houses, the person asking the question & the person or thing asked about are under duress, besieged
by untoward circumstances or beset by difficulties.
Something unfortunate in the past will lead to some
unhappiness or disappointment in the coming months.
In this chart, the Moon last passed over a benefic,
Jupiter, so what led up to this sale was very good;
she applies to the opposition of Jupiter which is a
separative aspect, good for giving up the carpet, &
especially good because she also parallels Jupiter.
A parallel means that the thing is as good as done.

The Moon or the angles (1st, 10th, 7th and 4th),
in cardinal Signs will conclude the matter quickly;
in fixed Signs, more time and expense are expected;
in common Signs, adjustments must be made, and more
time or many more meetings or papers will be needed.

The Moon's aspects

We use the Moon's APPLYING aspects only, as made
from the Sign she is in, & we list them beneath the
chart together with the original GMT as on page 100
and also the Greenwich time when she changed Signs.

To find where they begin, take the original GMT,
its date and hour-&-minute, which you are to locate
in the Aspectarian section at the back of the ephemeris. That is the starting-point for her aspects &
we list them in the order in which they are given,
using only the conjunction, sextile, square, trine,
opposition & especially the very powerful parallel.
We stop according to the time and date when she enters the next Sign - automatically leaving the Sign
she is in in the chart - as given in a Table at the
back of the ephemeris; for Raphael's it is on p. 39.

The more lunar aspects, the more activity to expect in the matter. If the majority are bad and if
the Moon conjuncts, squares or opposes Saturn there
will be many delays and obstacles. If the majority
are good but there are many of them there will be a
lot of shilly-shallying, coming-and-going and delay
to that extent.   In either case, the Moon's final
aspect tells whether the end is satisfactory or not.

There must be an aspect between the ruler of the
Ascendant (the inquirer) or the Moon and the planet
ruling the house of whatever is asked about, otherwise there is no action between them in the matter.
The Moon substitutes for either ruler if necessary.
In this chart, the inquirer-1st & the other-person-
7th will take action because their rulers, Moon and
Saturn, are in aspect. The 2nd House (possessions)
is ruled by Uranus who is aspected by the Moon; and
the other-person-7th ruled by the Moon will buy the
carpet, therefore, because there is activity there.

Squares denote difficulty, obstacles to overcome
and greater expenditure of energy.   There are none
in this chart.   Sextiles give an opportunity to get
whatever is wanted, as Moon sextile Uranus ruler of
the 2nd (possessions: the carpet).   The conjunction
brings co-operation if requested or needed.   Oppositions are separative but if the two planets are in
mutual reception with each other or if the inquirer
wishes to be rid of someone or something it may not
necessarily be bad; otherwise it denotes a pulling-
apart, separation or divorce, and jealousy or envy.
Trines signify success with ease, as in this chart.
The parallel is very strong & in a class by itself.

The parallel aspect

The parallel is based on declination as given in
the ephemeris for the planets along with longitude,
and is marked either North or South.   Two planets
within one degree of being the same in declination
are in parallel aspect, the greatest magnetic force
in astrology, attracting the one to the other.   The
parallel holds or lets go according to whether they
are both in the same declination-direction North or
South which acts like a conjunction that is lasting,
or whether one is North and the other South so that
the attraction ends in separation, as an opposition.

In questions joining the inquirer & another person as in marriage, partnership, friendship, buying
and selling, etc.; or the inquirer & something lost;
or the inquirer and whether he will accomplish whatever he is asking about (as a job, a trip, an education, etc.) if the Moon or the ruler of the Ascendant (the inquirer) parallels the ruler of the house
representing whatever is asked about, there will be
action between them & they will attract each other.
Whether that attraction holds or lets go depends on
whether they are in the same declination-direction.

which holds - or opposite, leading to a separation.
In this chart, the Moon is parallel all the planets
in the 9th House by opposite declination-direction,
attracting for the sale, letting go for the carpet.

If the Moon's final aspect is parallel a direct
planet it means "The thing is as good as done now".

The effects of the Moon's aspects

The first aspect the Moon applies to tells what
to expect first, & she gets off to either a good or
bad start according to the nature of that aspect.
In this chart, the Moon rules the buyer-7th and she
immediately aspects Saturn ruler of the seller-1st,
her first aspect, bringing the two together at once
& by trine, the good aspect signifying a good start.

Her final aspect reveals how the matter will end
and if bad it is very unsatisfactory, & the more so
if the planet is a malefic: if also retrograde, the
inquirer regrets the course he took & usually would
like to take back something he said.   If her final
aspect is good and the planet is direct, the matter
ends well as in this case: but if parallel a planet
retrograde the answer is "Yes: but not as expected:
it is as good as done now, but will come too late."

A poor beginning may thus end well, while a good
beginning may come to nothing. A bad beginning-and-
ending defeats the inquirer's purpose in every way.
In this chart, the Moon's first & final aspects are
good, thus the new student knows the answer at once.

If the Moon cannot complete her final aspect because the planet changes signs before she can reach
the necessary degree, one of the persons will abandon the matter before it can be finished or because
he thinks it cannot be accomplished & so backs out.

In questions involving two persons, the inquirer
and the one inquired about, their rulers are called
significators.   The one of these first aspected by
the Moon tells which person takes the first step or
makes overtures in the matter to introduce himself
or to present to the other whatever he has in mind.
In this chart, the Moon's first aspect is to Saturn
ruler of the inquirer who took the first step by advertising the carpet for sale: this is confirmed by
the ruler of the 1st in the 7th to show that he has
gone over to the other's side in search of a buyer.

If the ruler of the 7th is in the 1st, the buyer
has come in search of the seller. When each one is
in the other's house, two people are mutually seeking to meet each other; the planet they both aspect
represents a third person as an introductory agent.

The planet the Moon last passed over - no matter
how far back in the chart - was by conjunction & it
reveals what led up to asking the question: usually
related to something ruled by the house the planet
is in and conditioned by that planet's nature & the
good or bad aspect it is in. A malefic well placed
by Sign, direct in motion & not in the 1st House or
the house ruling the matter or person or thing that
is asked about, was not necessarily ill-disposed at
that time. Show the conjunction-symbol in brackets
first in line below the chart; it is a separation -
but if the Moon applies to it now it comes up again.

In this chart, the Moon last passed over Jupiter
in the 9th House of publishing trine Uranus in Gemini the Sign of advertising (a possession, since he
rules the 2nd House), accounting for the advertise-
ment to sell a carpet. That it would bring results
is shown by both Jupiter and Uranus sextile the Sun
in the buyer's money-2nd - and he bought the carpet
at 3:01 p.m. PST August 17, 1946 without quibbling.

The power of the planets.

Any lunar aspect at all to Saturn will delay the
proceedings to some extent at least. In this chart
it was by trine, therefore not unfavorable, & being
at the beginning of the list it was soon over & the
sale was consummated in two days.   Saturn aspected
late in the list delays the final consummation, and
withholds something, especially payment in full; in
this chart payment was made in full.   However, the
buyer's check was refused (Moon opposition Jupiter)
on the 16th; on the 17th (Moon trine Sun) he sent a
friend who brought payment in full in cash (because
the Moon's final aspect was then parallel Jupiter).

The Moon aspecting Mars operates quickly. If in
bad aspect there may be debate or argument (in this
case, her opposition caused a few words of argument
on refusing the check). Mars in the 1st or 12th is
likely to involve officials or police in the matter.

The Moon aspecting Uranus brings some unexpected
development or change; her good aspect in this case
protected the possession ruled by Uranus from being
threatened by a possibly-worthless check. Uranus in
the 1st in any horary chart denotes great vexation.

The Moon afflicting Neptune gives possibility of
fraud or deception, misinformation, unreliability &
disappointment. Her opposition in this chart could
have registered that way were it not for the saving
grace of their parallel. In good aspect, Neptune's
benefic side registers very much like that of Venus.

The Moon aspecting Pluto, ruler of groups, gives
dealings with unusual people - sometimes underworld
figures, subversives or gangs - often by proxy, due
to the absence of someone important in the case; in
this one, the buyer sent a friend with the payment.

Some significant clues

If Saturn is in the 1st House no satisfaction is
possible in the matter asked about: if he is retrograde there, he destroys every vestige of hope. If
he or any other malefic - Mars, Uranus, Neptune, or
Pluto - is in the 2nd House (which is the immediate
future) some trouble will soon arise & it generally
involves money, possessions, children, or some need
for self-protection. In the 3rd they cause trouble
regarding relatives, neighbors, gossip, messages or
non-deliveries. If in the 12th, trouble behind the
scenes; restraint, arrest, hospitalization, ambush,
waylaying, dealings with those in grief or in need.

If Mercury is retrograde or slowing down to turn
retrograde soon the plan either falls through or is
postponed, or someone changes his mind & backs out.
If Mercury is in good aspect to the Ascendant it is
sure to benefit the inquirer - but if in bad aspect
the failure or postponement of the matter is a disadvantage and he loses thereby. The Moon & Mercury
in bad aspect, even direct, denotes many annoyances.

If the ruler of the inquirer or the one inquired
about is retrograde, he is ill or worried & holding
something back or being evasive. If well placed by
Sign he is merely backward about taking active part
in the matter. If in 22 Leo he is not able to act
for himself or is not his own master. In the 29th
degree of any Sign he is at the end of his rope and
losing hope or patience. In 29 Taurus the place of
the Weeping Sisters, he has something to weep about.
In 24 Taurus, the headless Medusa, most evil of all
fixed stars, he "loses his head" about something or
someone connected with the question. In 19 Scorpio
the 'cursed degree of the accursed Sign, he makes a
lot of trouble for himself and others. In the same
degree as the nodes a casualty of some kind occurs.

The answer to your question

To sum it all up, your question can certainly be answered & you can know immediately what answer you will receive by observing the main rules of horary.

If the Moon is entirely void of course (not making any applying aspect at all from the Sign she is in) you know exactly what to say: nothing will happen and there is nothing to worry about. But if in aspect or parallel to an Arabian Point that relates to the type of question asked, then she is not void of course and there will be some activity to expect.

If Mercury is retrograde or about to be, someone in the case will engineer a change of mind or plan, or will postpone the whole matter. This will be of benefit to the inquirer if Mercury is in benefic aspect to the Ascendant: in bad aspect, it harms him. If the Moon is in bad aspect to Mercury, there will be many small annoyances, rewriting of documents or revising of opinions, and odd notions to counteract.

The way you start & finish will be shown at once by the Moon's first & last aspects; and also if she aims at an aspect that she can not complete because the planet moves out of the Sign before she reaches the necessary degree. You can tell what led up to asking the question by noting which planet the Moon last passed over and the matters ruled by the house it is in. And if you are dealing with someone else you can quickly tell which will take the first step or make overtures in whatever matter is asked about.

You know that a horary chart is set up as you do a birth chart because it is the birth of a question and only that first chart is good for that question.

✶ ✶ ✶ ✶ ✶

THE WAY OF

AN ELECTION CHART

THE   ELECTION   CHART

The right time to start an important action, sign
or file a document or enter into an agreement, etc.
is the best time attainable on the desired day, and
such an election chart as it is called may be based
on a natal chart or more expeditiously on a natural
wheel with 0-Aries rising & then turned accordingly
if the time is left open to choose the best aspects.

If the time is already set, as for an appointment
or departure by some type of conveyance & the usual
chart shows the circumstances to be unfavorable, it
is the part of wisdom to protect your own interests
or safety, changing the hour to one more propitious.

In a natural wheel with 0-Aries rising, enter the
planets from the ephemeris on the day decided upon,
or set several such wheels for a choice of days and
settle on the one with the most desirable planetary
features. Keep in mind the house governing the matter under consideration and turn the wheel to get a
trial Ascendant that is in good aspect to the Sign-
and-degree held by the ruler of that special house.

If the Sun appears in a house unsuitable by time
of day or night to begin the action, turn the wheel
accordingly until the Sun and Ascendant are acceptable; holding in mind the other safeguards, such as
keeping malefics out of angles because they afflict
the 1st House by conjunction, square or opposition.

In the Table of Houses, find the trial Ascendant
for the place's latitude, take its accompanying Midheaven and remaining cusps and show them in a trial
chart. The cusp the Sun is nearest denotes the approximate time for the chart and our starting-point.

Before doing that let us look at this chart for a
wedding that took place on Sept. 10, 1941 at 89W06,
42N16 at 3:00:00 p.m. CST - a most ill-chosen time.

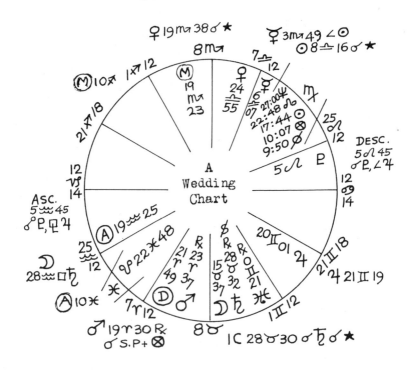

A Wedding Chart

In a marriage chart, the 4th reveals how and when
it is to end; which will be too soon for the happiness shown by the rulers of the 1st & 7th conjunct.
Saturn ruling the First House represents the groom,
afflicted by Uranus' conjunction and ill-starred by
conjunction to the Pleiades in the end-of-life-4th,
so that his early death would occur when progressed
4th reached Saturn in 21 years. He died suddenly &
unexpectedly on July 28, 1962 with Moon 28 Aquarius
exactly square Saturn, the Sun-ruler-8th conjoining
Vindemiatrix 8:41 Libra, Star of Widowhood; & Venus

on the accursèd degree 19 Scorpio conjunct the Part
of Marriage & thereby setting off its square to the
Part of Affection 19 Aquarius. The arc 21:00 moved
the Part/Marriage to 10 Sagittarius and the Part/Af-
fection to 10 Pisces, both badly aspecting the Part
of Mis-fortune (so-called when in the fatality-8th).

An 0-Aries trial wheel would put Mars in the 1st
opposition Venus in the 7th, these two representing
the groom and bride, separating them by quarreling.
Taurus rising would have the same rulers afflicted,
with two malefics in the 1st House this time.   But
Gemini rising would be good, with Jupiter 20 Gemini
in the 1st if we try say 15 Gemini on the Ascendant.
Note also that Jupiter governs this 7th-of-marriage
and is in good conjunction-aspect to this Ascendant.

In the Table of Houses & under Latitude 42 North,
we find an Ascendant 15:45 Gemini & MC 20 Aquarius.
In this wheel the Sun is near the 5th cusp denoting
10:00 p.m. CST Sept. 10th & that is where we start.

$$
\begin{array}{rl}
10:00:00 & \text{p.m. CST Sept, 10, 1941} \\
\not{}\quad 3:36 & \text{Diff for 89:06 W/Longit} \\
\hline
10:03:36 & \text{p.m. LMT-interval, 10th} \\
1:40 & \text{correction for interval} \\
0:59 & \text{correction EGMT 5:56:24} \\
\not{}\quad 11:16:31 & \text{S.T. previous noon 10th} \\
\hline
21:22:46 & \text{Trial Calculated S/Time}
\end{array}
$$

$$
\begin{array}{rl}
\text{from}\;\; 21:29:39 & \text{S.T. for MC 20 Aquarius} \\
00:06:53 & \text{later than 10 p.m. 10th} \\
\not{}\quad 10:00:00 & \text{trial p.m. CST Sept. 10} \\
\hline
10:06:53 & \text{p.m. CST 10th, MARRIAGE}
\end{array}
$$

10:06:53 p.m. CST ∤ 3:36 Diff. for 89W06 = 10:10:29
p.m. LMT 10th ∤ 5:56:24 EGMT = 16:07 (past midnight
so - 12:00 midnight = 4:07 a.m. GMT Sept 11th: this
subtracted from the coming noon 11:60 = 4835 C/Log.

Here we have no malefics in angular houses.   The
rulers of the 1st and 7th, Mercury and Jupiter, are
well aspected to each other and to Venus who trines
the Ascendant; not only that, but all of them trine
the Part of Fortune in the 9th for a happy ceremony.

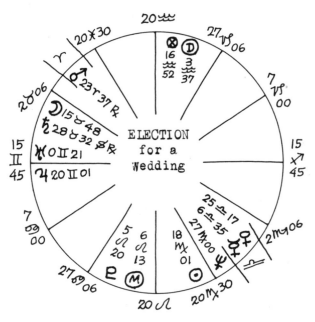

In this election the progressed 4th would not conjunct a malefic until it reached Neptune in approximately 37 years which would have permitted them 16
more years of happiness together.   In 1959 when the
progressed Sun reached Mercury in the children-5th,
they adopted a baby girl (Neptune in the 5th denies
children generally) also shown in the actual chart.
In 1965, 24 years after marriage and 3 years after
it ended, the arc 24:00 moved the Part of Deaths to
27:37 Aquarius square Saturn-ruler-mother-10th, and
the mother passed on.   Note (D) in the actual chart.

* * * * *

ASTROLOGY & CAESARIAN SECTION

This writer has come to the considered conclusion
that Caesarian Section could save the life of a new-
born infant whose natal planets would be very badly
afflicted on the expected day, if an astrologer had
the opportunity somewhat in advance of the impend-
ing birth to elect a safer hour of induced delivery.

Such an election chart will suppress the power of
malefic planets or malefic aspects from registering
in angular houses and thereby give the ruler of the
8th its SURGERY-instead-of-death reading if in good
aspect to the Ascendant. The identical aspects possible at normal birth may still be present at Caesarian Section but the house positions would be less
physical & thus more mundane in general application.

There are three immediately-apparent reasons for
advising Caesarian Section, based on the planetary
arrangement on the day of the expected birth, shown
in a natural wheel (one with 0-Aries rising). They
all have to do with the three Moons: the Natal Moon,
the Progressed Moon and the Birthday Moon - because
these forecast the coming year's principal activity.

If the Natal Moon is conjunct or opposition Neptune it presages trouble during the pre-natal period
that is physically evident at birth. If the Natal
Moon is moving forward to square a malefic she will
do so as a Progressed Moon on or before the seventh
birthday, and if the malefic is in an angle it will
be physically harmful then, seeing that these years
are susceptible to being afflicted during childhood.

The Birthday Moon is the transiting Moon in the
current ephemeris on the birthday anniversary each

year (not the Moon accompanying the Solar Return unless it falls on the birthday itself - which it frequently does not).   The first Birthday Moon to forecast a year in advance is the Natal Moon.   If the
Birthday Moon at birth or later happens to coincide
with a major transit in afflicting a planet ruling
or in the 8th House it signifies a time of danger &
the Progressed Moon will corroborate the occurrence.

For ourselves in particular, we look ahead each
year in the current ephemeris to ascertain what
our Birthday Moon will aspect, to designate the
YEAR to watch, during which period the month in
which the Progressed Moon makes a strong aspect
foretells the MONTH to watch; & the day of that
month when a major transit conjuncts or opposes
something in the chart is the approximate DAY.

Three lives that could have been saved

Our first two natal charts were chosen because of
having the same cusps although 17 years apart - the
girl living only 1½ hours, the boy 5½ years.   The
third natal chart is for a boy who lived 1½ years.

It may be no more than coincidental that all three
had Jupiter ruling the 8th and in bad aspect to Saturn; and intercepted Signs in the 12th & 6th Houses
to account in part for interference in their health.

On the opposite page is given the natal chart for
Linda who was due mid-morning of Feb. 3, 1949, born
at 10:45:00 a.m. PST, 118W15 34N03. Jupiter-ruler-
8th squares Neptune R in an Air Sign (suffocation),
and Linda was born with the cord twisted around her
throat, thus unable to breathe properly. Her brain
was denuded of oxygen (ruled by Mercury square Lil-
ith-of-childbirth in the throat Sign Taurus), & she
died at 00:14 p.m. PST that same day, aged 1½ hours.

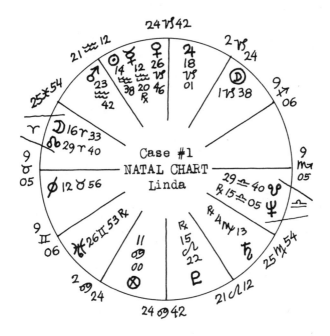

Case #1
NATAL CHART
Linda

We digress here to explain that pre-natal affliction is disclosed by the natal Moon conjunct or opposition Neptune at birth (because the natal Moon's
Sign-&-degree position is on the horizon for all of
the gestation charts, and slow-moving Neptune there
throughout the entire period will cause an abnormal
congenital (existing at birth) condition). In this
case it happened 9 days before birth when pre-natal
Mercury turned retrograde in 20 Aquarius, to be opposed by the solstice point of the natal Ascendant.
Transiting Lilith 15:55 Aries on the Moon activated
her opposition to Neptune, emphasizing the antagon-
ism Lilith harbors toward all children; the Moon in
26 Sagittarius opposed Uranus-the-non-conformist, &
Venus 15 Capricorn, ruler of the "future" Ascendant,
squared both the Moon & Neptune. These dire threats
alone would have cautioned us to advise a Caesarian.

Electing the time (Jacobson Method)

This method using the natural O-Aries wheel shows
Linda's Aries Moon in the 1st House opposition Neptune to endanger life during Caesarian Section, thus
the wheel must be turned to push her into the 12th.
Mars 23 Aquarius rules the surgery-8th: in the 11th
he could sextile the Ascendant for successful surgery if we have 23 Aries rising, the Moon then well-
placed in the hospital-12th. The Sun thus close to
the 11th cusp gives 10:00:00 a.m. PST as our starting point. For 23 Aries rising (34 N) the Sidereal
Time 19:00:49 gives 14 Capricorn for the Midheaven.

```
          10:00:00 a.m. PST Feb 3, 1949
     +     7:00 Diff for 118:15 West
          10:07:00 a.m. LMT Feb 3, 1949 *
     +  12:00:00 preceding noon, 2nd
          22:07:00 interval since noon
             3:41 correction, interval
             1:18 "    for EGMT 7:53:00
     +  20:49:23 S.T. prec. noon, 2nd
          19:01:22 Tentative Calc. S.T.

     -  19:00:49 S.T. MC 14 Capricorn
          00:00:33 earlier than 10 a.m.
   from 10:00:00 a.m. PST 3rd (trial)
           9:59:27 a.m. PST 3rd SURGERY

     +     7:00 Diff for 118:15 West
          10:06:27 a.m. LMT Feb 3, 1949 *
     +   7:53:00 EGMT for 118:15 West
           5:59 pm GMT 3rd = 6033 C/Log
```

This simple adjustment of planets using a natural
O-Aries wheel to get the ruler of the special house
in good aspect to the Ascendant as required (and no
malefics in angular houses) is successful in giving
the exact time for the beginning of any undertaking.

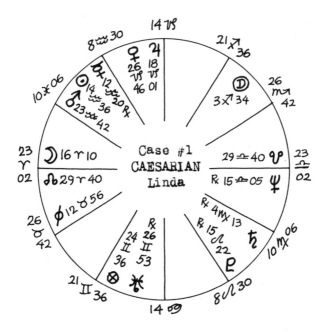

Case #1
CAESARIAN
Linda

In Linda's actual birth chart Uranus was quincunx Venus-ruler-Ascendant, an 8th-house aspect afflicting the body already struggling to breathe, and was also semisquare the Ascendant itself & Lilith there in the throat Sign Taurus, compounding the trouble.

In this Caesarian chart, Uranus conjunct the Part of Fortune and sextile the Ascendant brings success by modern methods to the body by surgery as denoted by his trine to Mars, ruler of the body-Ascendant & ruler of the 8th House of surgery; his good aspects outweighing his semisquare to Lilith in Taurus, the original strangling-conspirator in the first place.

Mercury (hands) square the natal Ascendant & Lilith in Taurus denotes an instrument birth, with the possibility of aiding-&-abetting the twisting cord.

On the opposite page is given the natal chart for
Lester who was due Sept. 18th, 1932 and was born at
7:50:00 p.m. PST that day, his chart & Linda's very
similar. His Moon does not conjunct or oppose Neptune, so there was no pre-natal trouble, but Jupiter
again rules the 8th, sesquares both Uranus & Saturn
for sudden & unexpected death and exactly conjuncts
Neptune for a mystery at death and Lester died very
unexpectedly on May 28, 1938, age 5½, cause unknown.

Any astrologer would have considered the T-square
Saturn-URANUS-Mars a serious threat, the more so because the Moon was moving to square its epicenter,
URANUS, from her month-by-month progressed position
22 Cancer in ≠5 days (years) measuring to May, 1938.
An eclipse list showed an eclipse in 7:32 Gemini on
May 28th that year semisquare URANUS, both eclipse
and Progressed Moon (conjunct the solstice point of
the eclipse 22 Cancer) activating the T-square into
spontaneous reaction. The eclipse was opposition &
parallel the Part of Death, square Neptune & square
Jupiter-ruler-death-8th, and he died that very day.

Since Linda died during her first year, her Natal
Moon was also her Birthday Moon threatening trouble
by opposition Neptune and square Jupiter-ruler-8th.
Lester's Birthday Moon 8 Pisces forecast a terrible
year ahead by opposition to Neptune, Jupiter-ruler-
8th, and the solstice point of URANUS and by square
to the eclipse and the Part of Death --- all exact.
Venus-ruler-Ascendant had progressed to exactly conjunct the solstice point of the Moon in the end-of-
life-4th House, to close their original bad aspect.

Before we can read early death in a chart we will
do well to make assurance doubly sure, as we did in
these examples, because the Part of Death by itself
is quiescent.   In an otherwise-protected chart, it
can mean only danger of death, etc. to someone else.

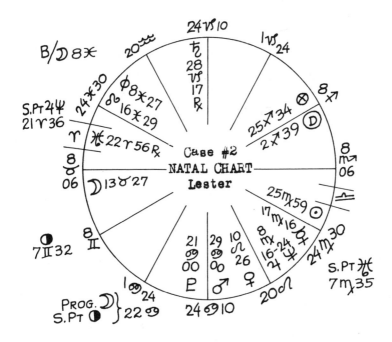

Case #2
NATAL CHART
Lester

An eclipse in good aspect to the Ascendant is not
without merit in an otherwise-fortunate natal chart,
being a harbinger of protection & compensation that
counteracts much of the trouble befalling the chart
by its bad aspects elsewhere. The effect registers
according to the people and matters generally ruled
by the houses thus afflicted, and since the Ascendant is well-aspected, the native will know about it.

Any election chart, and especially a Caesarian as
in this case, can be re-routed so as to deflect the
impetus away from the native so that what occurs in
his "circle" need not be a matter of life or death.

We want to break the power of this T-square therefore by getting Saturn & Mars out of angular houses
but keeping the eclipse favorable to the Ascendant.

In Lester's case, an O-Aries wheel puts his Aries
URANUS in the 1st (birth), setting off his T-square
involving Saturn and Mars. We want the benefics in
angles, the malefics subdued in cadent & succeedent
houses, and the eclipse rendered pointless by being
not conjunct or opposition anything but still well-
aspected to the Ascendant and especially trine from
its position 7:32 Gemini. Thus we want 8 Aquarius;
rising for 34 N, the MC 26 Scorpio (15:34:42 S.T.).

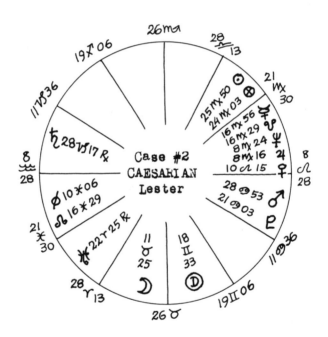

The Sun near the 8th cusp gives 4:00 p.m. PST for
our starting-point & the Trial Calc. S.T. 15:58:45,
which minus 15:34:42 S.T. for MC 26 Scorpio reveals
00:24:03 earlier than 4:00 p.m. or 3:35:57 p.m. PST
Sept. 18th for surgery. P.m. GMT 18th = 3157 C/Log.

We should always include the solstice point of an
eclipse in any chart because it registers even when
the eclipse itself may not - since the first office
of a solstice point is to ATTRACT ATTENTION. Here,
the solstice point 22 Cancer of the eclipse exactly
conjoins the Progressed Moon and attracts attention
to the nature of her aspect to Uranus which is evil.

In Lester's Caesarian chart on the opposite page,
the eclipse is not conjunct or opposition anything,
so any malefic aspect it makes is weaker because it
has no starting impetus, registering more as a very
strong lunation affecting him through the persons &
matters ruled by the house it is in, and protecting
him physically through good aspect to the Ascendant.

The lunation-effect of an eclipse

At Lester's age 5½ the eclipse falling in the 4th
unsettles the home and family and disturbs his year
ahead because it squares his Birthday Moon - but it
does not denote a death, not being within 5° orb of
aspect to the ruler of the death-8th house, Mercury.

What could it denote? It could mean a separation
from a parent since both natal and Caesarian charts
show that possibility by Moon square Venus ruler of
the home-4th or Venus in the home-4th. The eclipse
square Jupiter and Neptune in the lawsuit-7th could
precipitate a custody suit, separating him from one
of his parents.   This is also seen by his co-ruler
Saturn square the 9th cusp (legalizing of 7th-house
contracts) from the alienation-12th House & making
the separation aspect to Mars ruling the 10th House
(his standing in the community), at a time when the
solstice point of the eclipse & the Progressed Moon
join in squaring his other Ascendant-ruler, Uranus,
also retrograde to denote alienation or banishment.

The hylegiacal & anaretic points

The hylegiacal point in a natal chart reveals how
safe the native is.   The hylegiacal places are from
5° above the Ascendant to 25° below, the same opposite area for the Descendant, & the entire area from
5° below the 9th cusp to 25° below the 11th.   The
natal Sun or else the Moon in such an area is named
the Giver of Life; lacking these two, the Ascendant.

The Taker of Life or anaretic point is a malefic,
usually Saturn, Mars or Uranus; or the ruler of the
death-8th, even if it is a benefic but afflicted or
vulnerable to inescapable oncoming malefic aspects.

Linda's Sun was hyleg at birth but square the 1st
cusp (birth) denoting trouble at birth; Jupiter was
ruler of the death-8th House but anaretic by square
to malefic Neptune-of-suffocation. The Sun was also
hyleg in her Caesarian chart but protective by sextile to the Ascendant.   Lester's Moon was hyleg at
birth but on the Ascendant joining in its square to
its ruler Venus; Jupiter ruled his 8th, anaretic by
vulnerability to an inescapably-afflictive eclipse.
In his Caesarian chart the Ascendant is the hylegiacal point but protected from injury by the eclipse
which trined the Ascendant & had no starting-point.

Where Linda's chart showed death caused by a pre-
natal affliction when the cord became wound around
her throat in utero to strangle her at birth, & our
second chart showed Lester's vulnerability to major
affliction from an eclipse to the ruler of the 8th,
our third chart (for Leigh as given on the opposite
page) shows susceptibility to fatality when the Ascendant is the hylegiacal point (Giver of Life) conjunct a malefic or its equally-evil solstice point.
All of these charts confirm the reliability of the
Birthday Moon through her impact-and-dating powers.

Leigh was born near his expected time at 3:08 a.m.
PDST July 4, 1955 at 118W15 34N03, and it needs but
a glance to recognize the threat in his chart. The
Ascendant is hyleg and in only a year or so will be
conjunct the solstice points of two malefics, Uranus and Mars (both planets squaring Neptune-of-drugs
and conjunct Jupiter ruler of the death-8th House).

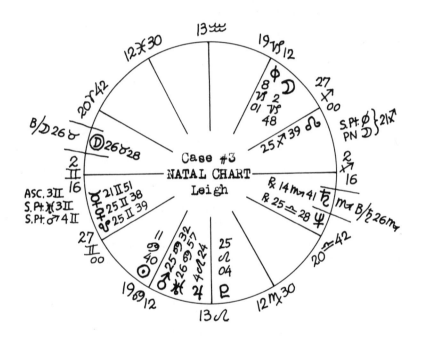

Case #3
NATAL CHART
Leigh

Going forward in the 1956 ephemeris for age 1,
his Birthday Moon the next year in 26 Taurus exactly conjoined the Part of Death (the Birthday Saturn
26 Scorpio being exactly opposite) as the pre-natal
Moon 21 Sagittarius opposed his Ascendant-ruler Mercury from her conjunction to the solstice point of
Lilith the dark moon harmful to children. At age 1½
Leigh caught a slight cold and was given penicillin
for the first time: he went into violent convulsion,
dying at 2:20 a.m. PST Dec. 20, 1956, cause unknown.

A natural O-Aries wheel would put the Sun, Mars & Uranus in the 4th & Neptune in the 7th, all angular & afflicting the 1st House. Turn it to put the Sun just above the 5th cusp for 10:00 p.m. PST July <u>3rd</u> trine the Ascendant early in Pisces (a closer trine would put Part of Death conjunct the mother-Moon) & the MC 13 Sagittarius (S.T. 16:46:16). 9:53:20 p.m. PST the corrected time (10:53:20 p.m. PDST surgery).

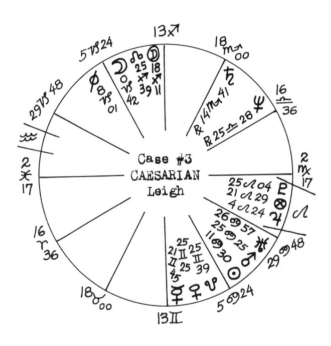

In this chart, the surgery-8th benefits the ruler of the Ascendant, Neptune, there, because a benefic Venus rules it & is protective when in an angle and especially trine to Neptune. The Moon and Jupiter are in mutual reception by house-rulership which is beneficial for both mother-Moon and native-Jupiter, co-ruled by this benefic well-placed in a Fire Sign.

✯ ✯ ✯ ✯ ✯

THE TWO FACES OF DANGER

Some of us bear a charmed life; we are the fortunate ones who escape unharmed in accidents that leave
others badly injured or worse. Either we have a protected natal chart that sees us through life without
much physical injury or we don't have Capricorn on
the 8th at birth and the Ascendant square a malefic,
or we don't start a journey under progressed aspects
that afflict the Ascendant or its ruler or a malefic
in the 1st or 8th House, or we don't board a vehicle
of any kind at a time when the chart set for its departure threatens either the craft or its passengers.

About Capricorn on the 8th: it has to do with the
Part of Peril, which we derive from the 1st plus the
ruler of the Sign on the 8th, then minus Saturn. If
Capricorn is on the 8th its ruler IS Saturn, meaning
that we add and subtract the same planet so that the
Part of Peril is exactly on the Ascendant ruling the
body itself, and if square a malefic planet the body
is sure to be injured in an accident at some time of
life.   Aware of this, the person whose chart it is
appeases the aspect by literally "watching his step"
so that he may sprain an ankle but not break a bone.

When we see a chart set for the time of departure
of an airliner such as the one on the following page
when all 84 people perished when it crashed into the
ocean, who can question the value of setting a chart
for every take-off of consequence so that the flight
can be delayed? Even if the planetary aspects remain
menacing we can still hold the ruler of the 8th cusp
of death at bay so that when the flight eventuates a
degree of appeasement is operative - to reduce major
danger to perhaps only a minor & non-fatal accident.

European Air Lines Disaster

6:31 p.m. EST, Feb. 8, 1965
Jones Beach
Long Island, N.Y. 73W40 41N36

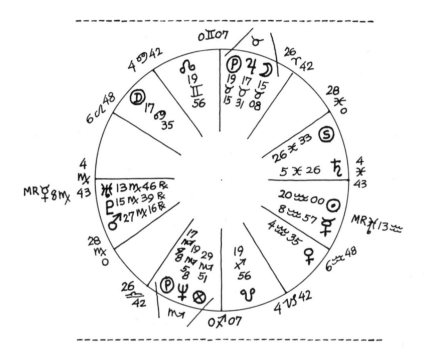

When Scorpio, Aquarius or Pisces is on the danger-
8th cusp as we see here, each having two rulers, Pluto and Mars, Uranus and Saturn, Neptune and Jupiter,
we have two Parts of Peril revealing double jeopardy
and thus two dangers to face.   In this tragedy, one
was explosion and the other drowning as shown by the
Moon (ruling the 11th of existing circumstances) who
carries the light from her trine to explosive Uranus
to her opposition of Neptune who rules drowning; and
this is confirmed by the Part of Death in the 11th &
in the Water Sign Cancer and Scorpio death-decanate.

In this chart there is a unique situation wherein
one ruler of the 8th, Neptune, is opposition its own
Part of Peril 19 Taurus, and the other ruler Jupiter
is opposition its own Part of Peril 17 Scorpio. The
Fixed Signs denote inevitable and inescapable danger
for this scheduled flight, clearly shown in advance.

The ruler of the 8th-of-death is called the Taker
of Life. Here, the two rulers Neptune & Jupiter are
in the 3rd and 9th travel-houses together with their
Parts of Peril, all of them intercepted so that they
would encounter interference en route; & one of them
in 19 Scorpio, given on p. 30 of Alan Leo's "Degrees
of the Zodiac" as the 'cursèd degree of the accursèd
Sign. In the same degree as the nodes, it involves
great misfortune, tragedy, and probability of death.

Conditions reach a crisis if the Critical Degrees
are prominent. They are 0-13-26 of Cardinal Signs,
9-21 of Fixed Signs, 4-17 of Common Signs. In this
chart, the travel-9th and the take-off Ascendant are
critical. Mercury rules the take-off: in only three
minutes he reached the critical 9th degree, disclosing that a crisis developed almost immediately, with
panic on board because three malefics are retrograde
in the 1st (passengers and crew) and he is in mutual
reception with Uranus, planet of emergency and panic.

The Part of Fortune in the 3rd cannot protect the
travelers. In Pisces or Scorpio or their decanates
or conjunct Neptune it is the Part of Mis-fortune; &
any planet or Arabian Point in 29 degrees is "at the
end of his rope" in despair of receiving assistance.
If Jupiter, Venus or the Part of Fortune had been in
the 1st, 10th, 7th or 4th some lives would have been
saved because benefics in angular houses do protect,
but no: this is a chart of double jeopardy with four
malefics in the angles and nothing in a self-reliant
Fire Sign excepting the always-morbid Part of Death.

The 10th-of-superiors is the house of the pilot,
represented by Mercury. The 6th-of-subordinates is
the house of the co-pilot represented by Uranus who
is retrograde in the 1st, also a member of the crew.
These two are in mutual reception denoting exchange
status, so that the pilot had taken the aircraft up
& then turned the controls over to the co-pilot Uranus who in the 1st House was in a leading position
thus piloting the plane at the time of the disaster.
Mercury in the 6th put the pilot in lesser position.

Uranus being at the controls gives him preferred
reading. Being retrograde denotes illness, particularly in Virgo-of-illness. The Saturnian decanate
shows a chronic condition. By mutual reception, he
is in 13 Aquarius in the 6th-of-illness, and square
Neptune who is susceptible to fainting, black-outs,
going into a coma, etc. The Moon rules the 11th of
existing circumstances and is opposition Neptune to
confirm possible loss of consciousness; and this is
further confirmed by the Sun (consciousness) square
Neptune. The Part of Sickness (1st plus acute-Mars
then minus chronic-Saturn) in 26:33 Pisces afflicts
Mars, denoting an acute attack of a chronic illness.

The question is: where did the misfortune arise?
We take the 12th-of-misfortune ruled by the Sun who
is in the sickness-6th square Neptune-the-comatose,
from the kidney-decanate of Libra, the Sign associated with the serious disease diabetes: it suggests
that the co-pilot Uranus fell into a diabetic coma,
losing control of the plane that exploded as it hit
the water, accounting for the double Parts of Peril.

How to avoid the worst

All of the foregoing ominous portents would have
alerted an astrologer to advise a take-off delay of
only 16 minutes. Aries would then be on the 8th &

the main danger would be averted, the Part of Peril
29:44 Pisces being at the end of its rope, past the
opposition of Mars-ruler-death-8th.   The Ascendant
and travel cusps would no longer be in critical degrees, nor would there be any interception to cause
interference with the journey en route, and no loss
of life.   And the Part of Fortune in 3 Sagittarius
conjunct the 4th would mean a fortunate homecoming.

Some hints for your safety

There are two charts to beware of: such a one as
afflicted as the disaster chart we have just read &
an afflicted election chart -- which is a chart set
for the desired beginning of a trip or other action.

Never start anything of importance when the time
would place Saturn in the 1st House of personal and
physical affairs.   He causes delay, frustration and
denial, thereby destroying all hopes of success and
pleasure in the undertaking: if he is stationary or
retrograde, everything comes to a standstill on the
one hand and there are unhappy repercussions on the
other.   In any chart at all, Saturn shows by house
where there will always be "the devil to pay" later.

If Mercury is retrograde, expect change of plan,
errors in documents, etc. and if the Moon is in any
cadent house (3rd, 6th, 9th, 12th) you may not land
where you planned.   And malefics angular upset you.

Any planet or Arabian Point in 29 degrees of any
Sign or conjunct 19 Scorpio, the 'cursed degree; or
24 Taurus, Caput Algol's fatal degree; or 29 Taurus
the place of the Pleiades or Weeping Sisters (which
gives you something to weep about) will harass you.
It is always better to have the Sun, Moon, ruler of
the Ascendant, & Part of Fortune above the horizon.

☆ ☆ ☆ ☆ ☆

THE WAY OF

AN INGRESS CHART

AS THE INGRESS GOES, SO GOES THE NATION

The longitude 00:00 of Greenwich makes that location the geographical & astronomical center of the
earth, and therefore the logical point of departure
for world affairs in general -- and these cover all
national, political and human interests such as the
state of the Nation and its governing head, war and
peace, import & export trade, foreign & domestic affairs, labor & management, the stock market, riots,
wide-spread disasters, epidemics, great discoveries
of economic, scientific and medical value, & developments of great universal as well as local benefit.

Greenwich is thus the logical & chosen location
for which we set "world charts" called ingresses of
which there are four. They mark the Sun's entry or
ingress into the four Cardinal Signs Aries, Cancer,
Libra & Capricorn each year, each ingress operating
for a period of three months, set for Greenwich and
called the London Ingress. It reflects world-wide
conditions in general and England's in particular,
and is the basic chart for ingresses anywhere else.

National charts set for the birth of a nation or
the building of state capitols, etc. are not always
dependable because of the margin for error in their
timing or difference in opinion as to the choice of
this or that as the most significant basis for such
a chart. In our own country, for instance, we have
no less than seven to consider astrologically, and
this diversity leads to a diversity in forecasting.

In national affairs it is an INGRESS chart that
not only proves itself dependable but does so within the 90 days of its three months' duration - and
this we shall demonstrate in this chapter, using a
London Chart adjusted to two other European places.

The Ingress Charts

The 4 Cardinal Signs give us the 4 cardinal directions N,E,W,S for the NEWS the four ingresses always
bring.   We want to know exactly when the Sun enters
0°00' of Aries, Cancer, Libra and Capricorn at Greenwich (0-Longitude, 52 N. Latitude) for the ingresses.

1.   Take the date when the Sun is nearest 00:00:00
of the required Sign.   The Difference will be in
minutes & seconds: mark the seconds C.   The difference in minutes is always 60/B.   Set down the
logarithm for each minute: their difference is A.
Multiply A by C and divide by B to find D, which
subtract from the log for the lesser minute, and
mark the result Log/Distance. Example: 3/20/1945

Required Sign 00:00:00 Aries was AFTER noon
Sun 3/20/1945 29:31:08 Pisces nearest at   "
Difference ..   28'52" between 28' = 1.7112 log
                    52/C   and 29' = 1.6960 log
A x C ÷ B = 131/D   60/B   152/A

Log Lesser Min. 1.7112 - 131/D = 1.6981 Log/Dist

---

2.   If the Sun was 0:00:00 BEFORE noon of that date
find his motion between that date & date before:
if it was 0:00:00 AFTER noon, take that date and
the date after.   Change the motion to Log/Motion.

Sun 3/21/1945 00:30:42 Aries
Sun 3/20/1945 29:31:08 Pisces
Motion ......   59'34" between 59' = 1.3875 log
                    34/C   and 60' = 1.3802 log
A x C ÷ B = 41/D   60/B   73/A

Log Lesser Min. 1.3875 - 41/D = 1.3834 Log/Motion

3. The Log/Distance minus the Log/Motion gives the
    Log/Time which will fall between a greater and a
    lesser logarithm pointing to 2 separate minutes,
    each having its log. The difference between the
    2 minutes is always 60/B; the difference between
    their logarithms is A.   The difference between
    the log for the lesser minute minus the Log/Time
    gives C. B x C ÷ A = D. The log for the lesser
    minute is also the Constant Logarithm for planet
    work. Change it to hours, minutes & 00 seconds,
    to which add D which results in the GMT/Interval.

```
  1.6981 Log/Distance
 -1.3834 Log/Motion
   .3147 Log Time ....... between .3151 C/L = 37'
                          and .3145 log = 38'
   .3151 Log Lesser Min            6/A      60/B
 - .3147 Log/Time
        4/C                     11:37:00 = .3151 log
                                +      40/D
  B x C ÷ A = 40"/D             11:37:40 pm GMT Int.
                 3151 C/L
```

----

4. If the ingress occurred AFTER noon, add the GMT
    Interval to 00:00:00 noon, and mark it p.m. LMT.
    If the ingress occurred BEFORE noon subtract the
    GMT Interval from noon (11:59:60); the result is
    then marked a.m. LMT; and in either case, dated.

```
  00:00:00 Noon March 20/1945
 +11:37:40 p.m. GMT Interval ........ .3151 C/Log
  11:37:40 p.m. LMT 3/20/1945
```

    Set the chart for 11:37:40 p.m. March 20th, 1945.
    Calculate the planets between March 20th & 21st,
    for Greenwich, Longitude 0:00, Latitude 52 North

The LONDON Ingress March 20, 1945

Our first step is to set the basic London Ingress Chart and from its Calc. Sid. Time set other charts.

On page 141 we find the data for the London Chart to be 11:37:40 p.m. LMT March 20, 1945, 0-Longitude & 52 North Latitude.   The GMT was p.m. of the 20th (planets between the 20th & 21st), the C. Log .3151

```
11:37:40 p.m. LMT 3/20      SUN 3/21, 00:30:42 Aries
       1:56 10" correction   3/20, 29:31:08 Pisces
23:50:37 Sid. Time 3/20                :59' = 1.3875
11:30:13 Calc. Sid/Time                   ⌐    .3151
                             3/20, ⌐ :29  = 1.7026
MOON 3/20, 2:12 Cancer      SUN 3/20, 00:00:00 Aries
```

For other cities

We take the Calc. Sid. Time from the London Chart and subtract the EGMT for West Longitude localities but add it for East Longitude localities, giving us the Calc. Sid. Time for the Ingress Chart elsewhere. In that place's chart thus found we enter the planets directly from the London Chart -- but each must show its own Part/Disaster (Asc ⌐ 8th cusp - Moon).

```
        11:30:13 Calc. S.T. for London
       - 5:08:03 EGMT Washington, 77-W
         6:22:15 Calc. S.T. WASHINGTON
                          39-N
```

```
11:30:13 Calc. ST London      11:30:13 Calc ST London
⌐ 6:01:35 EGMT Berlin 13E      ⌐ 5:57:59 EGMT Rome, 12E
17:31:48 Calc. ST BERLIN       17:38:12 Calc S.T. ROME
           52N30                          41N54
```

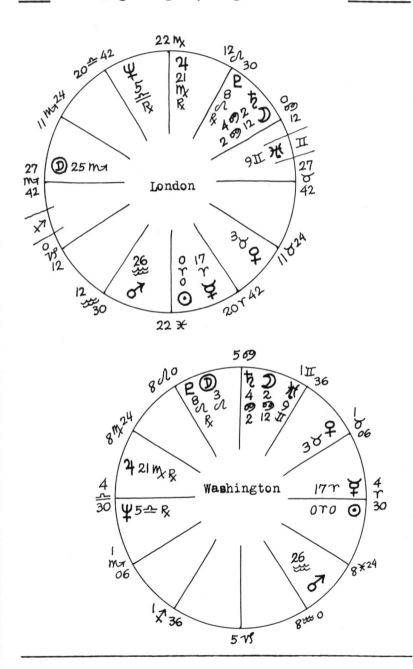

From the national point of view we look first to
the 10th House which has dual importance because it
represents the state of the Government and the condition of its representative king, queen, president
or other type of ruler. Always show the symbol (D)
for the Part of Death-or-Disaster or troubled times.

Here we see the planet of sorrow, Neptune, paramount in importance in the London Ingress (by being
in the 10th House) denoting a major death to happen
by square from the Moon in-and-ruling the death-8th,
confirmed by the Part of Death 25 Scorpio square to
Mars from the Mars-ruled funeral-12th. Astrologers
would note that the Moon rules this "World 8th" and
would thus expect her Sign Cancer to be prominent
in the ingress charts of other places due to suffer.

In our country, the Washington Ingress shows the
Sign Cancer on the 10th representing our Government
with the ruler Moon representing our President, and
badly afflicted by conjunction to Saturn, square to
Neptune and parallel Uranus who rules the 5th which
is the death-8th for anyone ruled by the 10th House.
At the same time, the (D) now in the 10th is square
Venus in-&-ruling the 8th, while the solstice point
26 Taurus of (D) falls in the 8th and squares Mars
in the 5th (President's 8th).   On April 12th, 1945
& within the 3-month ingress period from March 20th
to June 21st, our President Roosevelt died suddenly.

In 1945 there were two other national figures of
world-wide interest: Mussolini of Italy who was mur-
dered on March 28th, 1945 and Hitler of Germany, an
alleged suicide on April 29th, 1945 - both of these
also well within that March-to-June ingress period.

The Calc. S.T. being so close for Berlin & Rome,
we read the Berlin chart for both these men -- each
represented by the 10th House. Cancer is on the 5th,

their death-8th, with (D) there pointing to Jupiter
who rules the 10th and thus represents them. Death
would be violent as MARS rules this ingress-8th but
for Roosevelt it came gently with VENUS ruling that
ingress-8th. All three men would leave widows, due
to Sun square Moon and opposition the widow planet,
Neptune, who is conjunct Vindemiatrix, the "Star of
Widowhood" 8:41 Libra in separating aspect to Venus.

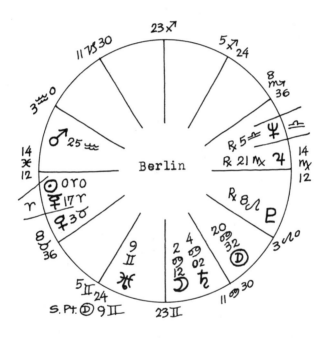

Mussolini and Hitler were not admirable figures,
the ruler-10th, Jupiter, being detrimented in Virgo
and square the Government-10th which represents the
honor of the populace-1st House. Roosevelt's ruler
Moon dignified in Cancer and conjunct the Midheaven
stood high in worldly esteem. Death in disgrace is
shown for Mussolini and Hitler, their ruler Jupiter
quincunx (death angle) Mars in the 12th-of-disgrace.

☿ ☿ ☿ ☿ ☿

THE MOVING FINGER WROTE "J.F.K."

Whether one believes in fatalism or not, one must
believe in mathematics - agreeing that its basis of
one-and-one-are-two is indisputable. What cannot
be disputed in mathematics must be acknowledged as
true and also as proof of the unvarying and certain
outcome of all the succeeding combinations. What is
certain to eventuate is thereby assuredly fatalistic because of its very certainty, & any student can
apply the rules and so prove the point for himself:
either our rules are dependable -- or they are not.

In astrology, mathematical distances between planets constitute aspects which, like a moving finger,
move on to certain & sure mathematical culmination
in an event or development in the native's circle -
no matter if he no longer lives at the time. Those
remaining in his circle continue to react to THEIR
aspects, in a manner of speaking.   It is no use to
hope that an aspect will operate against its nature:
a square will not register as a trine, nor can the
two parties to a conjunction register for good when
each of them is a malefic, nor for ill when each is
a benefic: in each instance they are two of a kind,
joining forces for or against.   The extent of the
good or evil delivered by any aspect is tempered according to the additional good or bad aspect it may
be involved in elsewhere. Thus we tell the difference between a mere threat & a foregone conclusion.

The reason for the inevitability of consequences
is simply that humans do not dispose. We can only
write down in the chart what the Moving Finger has
written in the heavens to be obeyed - and who among

us shall stay that Hand or presume to dictate to the
Deity? Not even the President of the United States.

> The Moving Finger writes: and having writ,
> Moves on; nor all your piety nor wit
> Shall lure it back to cancel half a line,
> Nor all your tears wash out a word of it.
>   Omar Khayyam

Reading a natal chart is a personal thing; you may
believe entirely in "personal free will" even though
what happened was contrary, and moreover was clearly
shown in advance, according to Sri Khayyam & others.
It is an inescapable conclusion that what took place
was fatalistic because it took place with or without
free will, and especially if it resulted in tragedy.

When the event is of national import or the person
is a national figure, an ingress chart will disclose
the situation more clearly than the natal chart, because the latter may not be correct or dependable in
one way or another, whereas the ingress chart is not
only surer to be correct but proves itself in ninety
days' time (its three-month period of being in force
as explained on page 139 herein) and since the chart
can be set as long as years ahead, it provides ample
warning in advance if indeed that can stay the Hand.

The four Ingress Charts each year mark the ingress
(entry) of the Sun into Aries, Cancer, Libra & Capricorn. They are of primary national importance since
they alone reveal what is to occur during the admin-
istration and we always look first to the 10th House
to see the "state of the Union", which is to say the
Country, the Government and its main representative,
the President. In this chapter we present the chart
for the Libra Ingress September 23, 1963, originally
set for 18:31:25 Calculated Sidereal Time for London
and adjusted to Washington, D.C. 77 West & 39 North.

The Libra Ingress Sept. 23, 1963

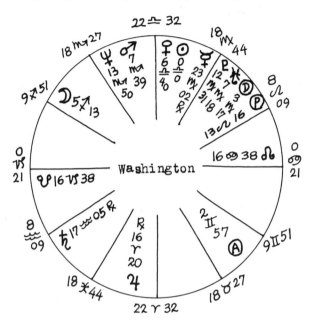

22 ♎ 32

Washington

It needs but a glance at the 10th House to understand what threatens the President. Mars & Neptune
conjunct are the classic signature of assassination
which is sure to eventuate because square Saturn in
Fixed Signs and in mutual application to the aspect,
with Neptune squaring the Part of Peril in the 8th,
& more definitely with the Part of Death in the 8th
squared by the Part of Assassination in 2:51 Gemini
in the 5th, the death-8th for the presidential-10th.
        (See p. 62 for Part of Assassination)
Thus the worst happened within 60 days on Nov. 22nd
when our President John F. Kennedy was assassinated.
What the Moving Finger writes is as unalterable as
the laws of the Medes & Persians, and when you find
a combination of malefic planets in evil aspect and
fixity by Sign, confirmed by malefic Arabian Points
you know the forecast will be death within 90 days.

Clues given by the Sun

In passing, the Sun in an ingress chart gives several clues that every student will find worthwhile, and which are in evidence in this case. The Sun at ingress is always 0-degrees and if the Ascendant is also in 0 degrees they are in exact aspect, portending developments in the ensuing 3-month period that will be more than ordinarily important; not only to the people of our nation (the Ascendant) but to the people of other nations also, as represented by the other end of the horizon, the Descendant, which the Sun automatically also aspects. If the aspects are good, such as a trine to one and sextile the other, better times are in store all the way around. But the square aspect means loss and disaster to us and also to other nations; and if the Sun's Sign Leo is on the death-8th cusp it augurs great loss of life.

This ingress Sun does square the horizon and does rule the 8th House accounting for the loss by death of our President and loss of life in the disastrous hurricane in Cuba and in the disastrous breaking of dams in Italy and California, all within the three-month ingress period. These Sun clues also confirm the assassination-significance of the Sun-ruler-8th semisquare Neptune in the presidential-10th as well as the Moon square both Uranus & the Part of Deaths 3:17 Virgo in the 8th which alerted alarmed astrologers to immediately examine the President's natal chart, & which we now present on the opposite page.

Planets changing in direction

When you set up a natal chart be sure to list any planets that change direction so many days after or before birth, denoting that many years after birth for noteworthy CHANGES in the life according to the promises or threats contained in the chart at birth.

The 10th is the house of Fate. Mr. Kennedy's has
Neptune there & badly conditioned by being conjunct
3:43 Leo, the midpoint between the Moon and Part of
Death 20:13 Gemini, and exactly semisquare the Moon
and waiting (in a Fixed Sign) for a progression to
set off the Moon's square to the Part of Death & to
Venus-ruler-Ascendant who is unfortunate in the 8th
House and "marked for death" by conjunction to (D).

3:15:28 p.m. LMT May 29, 1917, 71W08 42N05

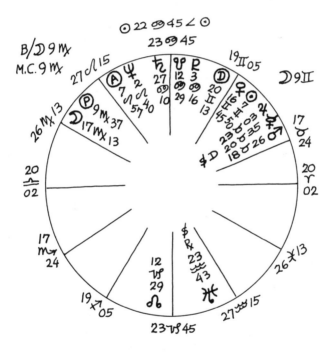

That wait was over when pre-natal Neptune 46 days
before birth (denoting 46 years after or 1963) went
direct in 2:05 Leo conjunct himself, accompanied by
progressed Saturn-of-Time, thus activating the Moon
into closing the diabolic midpoint-threat at birth.

The power of a mutual reception

It needs the combined force of several afflictive progressions to take the life and overcome the saving grace attributed to a mutual reception shown by two planets each in the other's natural Sign, which in this writer's opinion gives exchange status that allows each planet to be also read as though in its own Sign again, still carrying its same degree, and giving the native a way out of trouble if he wishes to get out of what he got into: he has that choice.

In Mr. Kennedy's chart, his ruler Venus is in the 8th-of-danger in mutual reception with Mercury also in the 8th. Unfortunately, this reads Mercury back in Gemini 20, conjunct the Part of Death: and Venus back in Taurus 16 conjunct the 8th cusp so that the mutual reception lost saving grace in the death-8th.

When Mr. Kennedy became President he assumed in a way whatever was to be active in the ingress charts for the Nation he represented. The combined indic- ations in the ingress chart & his progressions were fatalistic because progressed Mars exactly conjunct the Part of Death overwhelmed mutual-reception Mer- cury there, Mars being the stronger & also the same tenor as the Part of Death. Mercury is the planet by nature susceptible to outside pressure and influ- ence, exactly like the metal mercury that he rules, unable to resist Mars, ruler of the open-enemy-7th, so that violent death at another's hands took place.

The Moons to consider

There are several Moons to consider when progress- ing an afflicted chart: the natal & progressed Moon, the age-arc Moon and the Birthday Moon (the transit- ing Moon on his birthday in 1963). Some also take the transiting Moon on the day of the event but the

preceding lunation is generally more revealing, and
also possesses forecasting power.   We have already
seen the semisquare to the NATAL Moon from the pre-
natal Neptune & Progressed Saturn.   The PROGRESSED
Moon 9 Gemini in the 8th semisquared the Midheaven,
squared the progressed Midheaven, the BIRTHDAY Moon
and the natal Part of Peril all in 9 Virgo & in the
11th House of circumstances that were perilous from
birth because PERIL was always there & sesquare the
end-of-life-4th.   The arc 46° gave the natal Moon 4
bad aspects, moving her to 3 Scorpio square natal &
pre-natal Neptune & progressed Saturn & also 3 Leo,
activating her own midpoint with the Part of Death.

The preceding lunation

The Sun is the Giver of Life in this chart, being
in a hylegiacal position, but his solstice point in
22:10 Cancer conjuncts the Fate-Midheaven, throwing
back a bad semisquare-aspect to himself in the 8th.
At death his progressed Sun 22:45 Cancer & prenatal
Saturn 23:58 Cancer conjoined both solstice point &
Midheaven in their semisquare to the Sun in the 8th
to take his life -- but here is where the preceding
lunation proves its value: it occurred on Nov. 16th
in 23 Scorpio, and though it exactly squared Uranus
in the 4th (life ends suddenly) and was opposition
Jupiter in the 8th, it brought Mr. Kennedy probably
the greatest outpouring of love & honors that this
country has ever seen, because it also exactly paralleled Jupiter and trined the Midheaven as well as
the progressed Sun and pre-natal Saturn there.   If
there could ever be a measure of recompense for the
tragedy of death by assassination, this must be it.

Uranus-the-unexpected retrograde in the 4th turns
direct after Mr. Kennedy's death presaging a change
of burial place & of opinion concerning his murder.

★ ★ ★ ★ ★

THE DARK MOON LILITH OVERHEAD

When events of significance are to take place in our country within a three-month period as revealed in an ingress chart set for Washington, D.C. we can examine the progressed incorporation charts for our larger cities and thus seek to determine which will be the probable one in which the event is to happen so that it can be warned if disaster is approaching.

There is something mysterious about the unknown, especially when the aspects are foreboding, so that in such cases the dark moon Lilith is often suspect because of her mysterious and sinister nature. Her very presence in any kind of chart is an affliction. Her symbol is ϕ -- a lesser moon diagonally divided.

Lilith's nature is always betraying, compulsive, afflictive, abnormal, catastrophic, chaotic and con-dition-disturbing, poisoning, abortive, often fatal because of her malevolence, illicit & demoralizing. In the end, the trouble she causes involves a loss.

Lilith in a natal chart

In a natal chart she upsets the matters & people of the house she is in, the more noticeable if bad-ly aspected at birth (a lifelong effect) or by pro-gression (for that year) or by transit (for a day).

If angular her menace is physical (1st House) or domestic (4th); because of a partner or open enemy, (7th); an employer, or due to a parent's misfortune (10th). Succeedent, the loss involves money & pos-sessions (2nd); speculation, community property and children (5th); debts, taxes, settlement, alimony & legacy (8th); wages & dues (11th). Cadent, trouble

involving relatives, communications, rumors, travel
and deliveries (3rd); illness, tenancy, service and
trouble with small animals (6th) or with strangers,
in-laws, insurance, rituals or journeys (9th).   In
the unfortunate 12th House, the trouble arises from
mistakes, errors of judgment & restraint of freedom.

Lilith is considered to be exalted in Gemini and
thereby in her fall in Sagittarius, no Sign dignity
being allotted to her as yet.   When intercepted in
any chart she is shorn of some of her power for the
time being - especially in angular houses where she
otherwise operates early in life; still later if in
succeedent houses, and much later in life if in the
cadent houses - but she is waiting; biding her time.

Finding Lilith's position in the chart

For those unacquainted with this disturbing dark
moon, let us first illustrate how very simple it is
to find her Sign-and-degree position for any day of
the year.   In this writer's THE DARK MOON LILITH IN
ASTROLOGY her ephemeris is given from 1860 to 2000,
for the first of each month, always direct at 3°02'
per day.   Here are her monthly listings for 1966:

Jan	Feb	Mar	Apr	May	June
28Aqu13	2Gem07	27Leo03	00Sag57	1 Pi 51	5Gem45

July	Aug	Sept	Oct	Nov	Dec
5Vir57	9Sag11	12 Pi 35	12Gem38	15Vir51	16Sag12

To find her position on any other date, take the
difference-in-days, multiply it separately first by
2 for the minutes, then by 3 for the degrees, & add
them to her place on the 1st. If the result exceeds
30 degrees, subtract the Sign she is in and as many
more as necessary as exampled on the opposite page.

Lilith June 21, 1966 (21 - 1 = 20 days' difference)

```
        Lilith on June 1st, 1966 ......  5:45 Gem
        20 days (20 x 2' then x 3°) ... 60:40
                 (2 Signs too many) ... 66:25
        Subtract Gemini and Cancer .... 60:00
        Transiting Lilith June 21st ...  6:25 Leo
```

For 6:25 Leo, her Solstice Point is 23:35 Taurus.
3°02' is taken as her yearly motion by progression.

An Ingress Chart for our Country

The 4 ingress charts are set for the Sun's entry
into the Cardinal Signs Aries, Cancer, Libra & Capricorn, this one set for our Capitol at Washington,
D.C., 77-W 39-N, 3:33 p.m. EST June 21st, 1966; the
Cancer Ingress, for which we found Lilith 6:25 Leo.

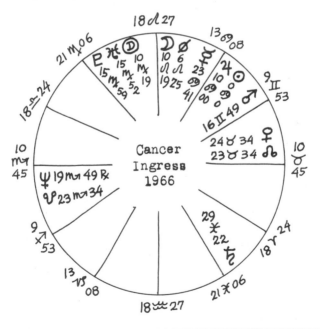

In a national ingress chart the 10th is taken as
the Ascendant for the First House of the Government
and its representative president, king, queen, etc.
but when adjusted to the longitude and latitude for
another locality, the 10th represents a State & its
governor or a city and its mayor.   The 5th is read
as the disaster-or-death-8th House for these rulers
counting forward from the 10th; the 3rd being their
illness-6th.   The 1st House represents the populace
or common people who take first place because without them we would have no nation per se; thus their
house of disaster-or-death is the 8th House itself.
The 4th House is the National homeland, the State's
confines or the city's limits in their own ingress.

Each of the four ingress charts is in force over
a three-month period; this one lasts from June 21st
to September 23rd, 1966.   Between these two dates
there is to take place an event that will be unfortunate due to house positions & evil aspects, & will
be inescapable because of the Moon and angles being
fixed by Sign.   It will shock the people because of
the planet of shock, Neptune, being in their house,
and will involve numerous deaths among them because
their ruler Mars is dual by Sign & in the death-8th.

At first glance we might fear for the President
because the Sun-ruler-10th is in the danger-8th
but his mutual reception with the Moon gets him
safely out of the 8th and back in his own Sign,
0 Leo in the 9th.   Cadent houses have delaying
action - and the mutual reception Moon protects
him by conjunction to Jupiter.   The Sun is not
"well" in Cancer, however, and his Part of Sickness (the 10th plus Mars, then minus Saturn) is
in 5:54 Scorpio square Lilith in Fixed Signs so
the President is not as well as we would desire.
(Since first writing this as a magazine article,
note his surgery during the following ingress.)

We always look first to see if all is to be well for the ingress period. Jupiter, Venus, Fortuna or any of their dispositors in the 10th actually or by mutual reception will give protection in adversity. Mercury the easily-adaptable planet, is convertible and if strong by Sign, direct, and not ruler of the 8th or 5th (the danger houses for the president and populace) he is considered a benefic; if retrograde or intercepted he will suppress news & information.

If the Moon is in the 5th or 9th her aspects (for greatest good or greatest evil) are short of totality because her end-of-the-matter 4th House will be the undependable 8th and 12th. If by mutual reception she can also be read in the 8th, 5th or 12th - as in this ingress - she still registers misfortune. The nature of the good or bad planet or point that she last passed over & the one she next passes over reveals what she picks up and will express. In this ingress she last passed over Lilith and next passes over the Part of Death so she is between two evils.

If the Sun rules the 10th and is not in the 8th, 5th or 12th badly afflicted, important governmental developments occur to our advantage. If in mutual reception or intercepted the worst can be postponed.

Malefics or the Part of Disaster-or-Death (which is 10 Virgo here) in the 10th afflicted or not, can bring serious troubles to the Government, according to the house in which the ruler of the 10th appears. Mars afflicted in the 7th threatens war or lawsuits affecting the Government or its respected officials.

The Part of Peril

If Capricorn is on the 8th cusp we find the Part of Peril (page 131) exactly conjunct the Ascendant, & if square a malefic serious accidents will occur.

The Ingress for Washington

For the Nation, the 10th is afflicted by malefic
Uranus and Pluto there, square Mars in the 8th; and
the Part of Death-or-Disaster also there & not only
exactly aspected by the Moon but the first she will
pass over, denoting major deaths during this three-
month ingress period. These are to occur among the
people at large because both Moon and Part of Death
are in exact aspect to the Ascendant (their house),
where the assassinating planet Neptune appears, ill-
starred by exact conjunction to the 'cursed degree.
We also note that Mars rules the people and is in a
dual Sign in their own death-8th House and squaring
the Part of Death & Uranus who strikes without warning, & Pluto who rules those congregated in groups.
From the forecasting point of view, this ingress is
one of the easiest-read examples anybody could ask.

When will it happen?

Within the 3-month ingress period the first date
of consequence is July 10th when the Moon conjuncts
19 Aries, the Solstice Point of (D), and Mars ruler
population-1st in 29 Gemini squares Saturn (and his
then Solstice Point 0 Cancer reaches the Sun in the
danger-8th House). Mercury-ruler-8th in 10 Leo will
conjunct the Moon and square the Ascendant and also
semisextile the Part of Death; so that the disaster
could take shape then or within a week with the oncoming lunation on Mercury himself, ruler death-8th.

Where will it happen?

This is a matter of pinpointing a locality which
is best done by keeping in touch with the charts of
our larger cities and their current progressed condition -- a task for the astrologer who specializes
in this department. Otherwise we must wait for the

event to happen, then adjust the Washington Ingress
to that other locality to find what accounted for a
major event there. This we will do now, to account
for the mass murder of 8 student nurses in Chicago
on July 14, 1966, between the two dates of ingress.

This Washington Ingress Sidereal Time is 9:23:23
from which we subtract the EGMT for localities west
of Washington but add if east of Washington.   This
gives us the Sidereal Time for an ingress elsewhere.
We use the planets as in the Washington Ingress but
give each new ingress its own Fortuna & Part/Death.

The ingress work for Chicago

```
 9:23:23 Sid. Time for Washington
-5:50:36 EGMT Chicago (west of ")
 3:32:47 Sid. Time Chicago Ingress
                  87W39, 41N52
```

Within the same 3-month ingress period there occurred another mass-assassination, on Aug. 1st when
14 persons were shot on the street in Austin, Texas.

Repeat the above process to find the Austin Ingress.

The ingress work for Austin

```
 9:23:23 Sid. Time for Washington
-6:30:56 EGMT Austin (west of  ")
 2:52:27 Sid. Time Austin Ingress
                  97W44, 30N16
```

These two ingress charts are given on the next page.

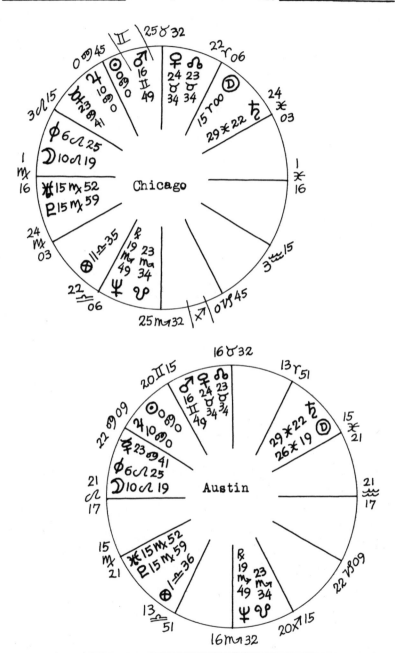

In each of these charts we find the dark moon in
the 12th House of waylaying-&-assassination because
these are the attributes of its natural ruler Neptune, confirmed by his Sign Pisces on the death-8th.

In each 8th House we see its own Part of Deaths,
also Saturn-the-Reaper whose solstice point O Libra
exactly squares the Sun while Lilith's is on Venus,
ruler of the 10th House of Fate in which Mars ruler
of the end-of-life 4th appears in a dual Sign denoting several deaths. If we had set an ingress chart
for every large city in the country these two would
have mirrored what the Washington Ingress foretold.

Even the Part of Fortune was unfortunate here by
being opposition the Part of Death in Chicago - and
conjunct the solstice point of the Part of Death in
Austin.   Venus rules the Sign the Parts of Fortune
are in but she is conjunct Caput Algol in 24 Taurus
who is the most evil of all fixed stars, and become
murderous here by parallel to Neptune-the-assassin
in the 'cursed degree (meaning A TERROR TO SOCIETY,
according to p. 30 of Leo's Degrees of the Zodiac).

In Chicago, the nurses were at a disadvantage in
hoping to save themselves because Mercury who ruled
their house was in the same degree as the nodes (to
denote a casualty or fatality). He went retrograde
that day, so they weakly obeyed the killer's orders.

In Austin, the Ascendant conjunct 22 Leo has the
meaning of "one who is not his own master", one who
cannot rule his life as he would if he could - & in
this tragedy his ruler Sun in 0° of a Cardinal Sign
is read as in a critical degree that brings matters
to a crisis, a point where he cannot save his life.
The fixity in the Washington chart showed all this.

✷ ✷ ✷ ✷ ✷

THE WAY OF

FORECASTING

THE BASIS OF FORECASTING

To forecast is to state in advance what the result of progressed planetary aspects will be in the life of the person whose chart it is. This is easier to do if we keep in mind the known effects that became established rules in past progressions, remembering that the nature of the aspect is combined with that of the planet making it because they work together.

A good aspect such as a conjunction or parallel, a sextile or trine, means that the benefic or malefic planet making it is expressing its positive side in steering the native toward gain or success. A bad aspect such as a square, semisquare, sesquare, quincunx or opposition uses the planet's negative side, benefic or malefic as may be, so that the native is inclined to take the hard way or the wrong way now. Good and bad aspects operating simultaneously bring mixed blessings with success attended by some loss.

The Sun, for example, can be kind or cruel. Venus can be moral or immoral. Jupiter can give you much or too much for your own good. Saturn can give you time & patience now to concentrate on your goal, or duty or responsibility that delays whatever you do. Mars can bring great enterprise or foolish and rash self-application causing overwork, trouble and loss. Neptune's good side is inspirational and idealistic but his negative side is self-defrauding & chaotic, when by age-arc he progresses to an aspect bringing unexpected good luck or else some form of treachery.

Mercury's positive side increases knowledge & also capacity to use it now, to circulate freely in many different ways; his negative side limits all these, besides making the native susceptible to persuasion leading to errors of judgment and various mistakes.

A favorable aspect from Uranus directed by age-arc
brings unexpected developments affecting the status
quo, freeing the native in some way to take on some
personal interest, alliance or membership - usually
by asserting his independence; often bringing him a
windfall that improves his circumstances.   His bad
aspect disrupts his present circumstances and shows
departure from the norm in general, broken ties and
separations, unbonded relationships & lost friends.

Pluto's good aspects when directed by age-arc generally involve group activity, private dealings and
behind-the-scenes cooperation that works favorably.
His negative side brings out activities undesirable
from the personal, social or legal angle and always
complicates the life somewhat from then on due to a
continuing regret for complicating his life himself.

The Moon brings changing conditions, of the nature
of the house she is in and that of the houses holding the planets she aspects during her two or three
years' stay. She "carries the light" of her aspect
from there to her next aspect to the same planet so
that it is important to date that next aspect for a
future forecast. Any aspect she makes now, good or
bad, comes to fruition at that time; the change she
began develops into an event, and it will be of the
nature of whatever is signified by that next house.

Be sure to note whether the Moon makes her aspects
by moving forward to the planets or away from them.
Her forward sextile to a planet is followed by conjunction; an opportunity now reached. Her backward
sextile is followed by a square; an opportunity now
possible only by dint of extreme effort -- or lost.

In the same way, the Moon's aspects to the Arabian
Points (Fortuna, Marriage, Death, etc.) forecast an
eventuality or development related to their nature.

Aspects

It is efficient to figure the whole life ahead, so
far as progressions indicate, so that favorable and
unfavorable periods can find us prepared beforehand
to take advantage of good opportunities or be ready
to meet trouble mentally, financially or as needed.

The student may wish to study the chapter WHEN AND
HOW PROGRESSIONS OPERATE, p. 141, in this writer's
"Here & There in Astrology" for approximate timing.
The progressed aspect tells the YEAR, the month-by-
month progressed Moon the MONTH, a strong lunation,
eclipse or configuration of transits the DAY itself.

What occurs does not always involve the native directly and in fact will not unless the progressed aspect is directed to any angular cusp (because these
affect the 1st House) or to the ruler of the rising
Sign or a planet in any angular house because these
are in mundane relationship (house only) to the 1st.
Without such direct impact on the native, an aspect
mainly affects only matters or people in his circle
according to the house indicated & he becomes aware
of it sooner or later because succeedent or cadent.

It helps to recognize the import of an aspect when
we recall that it is based on distance from the 1st
cusp no matter where it occurs, at birth or by progression. The CONJUNCTION is always personal & co-
operative because it relates to the 1st cusp itself
representing the native personally. It is the most
basic of all aspects, and in forecasting you always
look for it first as the surest promise of activity
requiring the native's participation if it aspects
the Ascendant, its ruler or a planet in the 1st; or
involving matters & people important in his circle.
If the conjunction sets off a trine elsewhere you
forecast easy gain -- if sextile, an opportunity to

gain; if semisquare or sesquare, some unfavorable involvement with finances, present circumstances, unbonded relationships and whatever else is ruled by the succeedent houses - because they are those containing these midpoint aspects.   If quincunx, reorganization of the affairs because of illness, tenancy, absence or seclusion, travel, education, or whatever else is denoted by cadent houses, seeing that the quincunx measures to the cadent 6th. It also measures to the Ascendant from the 8th so that reorganization of the affairs could be necessary because of a debt, taxes, surgery or a death.

The SEMISEXTILE measures from the Ascendant to the cusp of the 2nd and 12th Houses and is minor in its impact and thus promises minor activity, but has to do with a slightly favorable opportunity to gain by financial or other assistance to or from others and by taking advantage of an opportunity for self-protective guarding of one's interests when in trouble.

The SEXTILE measures to the 3rd and 11th cusps and forecasts a favorable opportunity to gain by taking part in matters relating to travel, advertising and communication, relatives and neighbors, friends and memberships, and in achieving one's hopes & wishes.

If the planet being aspected is retrograde, there will be reluctance to taking advantage of the sextile: the person will not reflect his advantages, thus could not gain by the proffered opportunity.

The SQUARE measures to the 10th and 4th cusps, the meridian itself, ruling career, success, reputation and the mother; also the domestic environment & the home, real estate, family in general and the father. These house-rulerships are interchangeable, so that what happens to the career, reputation or mother is keenly felt by the family - and what happens in the

family or to the father affects the reputation, the
career and one's success in general.   These houses
square the personal 1st House, thus ANY unfavorable
development by square upsets the native's outlook &
environment during a period of trouble or discredit.

If aspecting a malefic it emphasizes fear & worry
and signifies an illness - sometimes an accident.
If aspecting a benefic it mitigates any trouble &
brings recompense for loss & some merited reward.

The TRINE measures to the 5th and 9th cusps and is
the most favorable aspect of all, bringing gain and
happiness with little or no effort from the native.
It forecasts a development involving something that
is speculative in the way it could turn out and may
come from hitherto-unknown persons, distant places,
social contacts or unexpected benefit thru a child.

If simultaneously square, semisquare or sesquare,
some loss accompanies the gain or some effort may
be required, or time lost before profiting by it.

The SESQUARE measures to the middle of the 5th and
9th Houses and is unfavorable as regards matters or
persons of those houses during the forecast period.
It could result in estrangement, disappointment concerning creative work, speculation, gambling, insurance, publications, school or church and traveling.

The QUINCUNX measures to the 6th and 8th cusps and
demands reorganization of the affairs because of an
illness or a death in the circle, or demand for tax
or other payments such as a debt, alimony or settlement or fee, & often a change in routine or tenancy.

The OPPOSITION measures to the 7th cusp, forecasting activity with another person involving partnership, marriage, contracts, etc., in which the other

person has equal rights with the native so that the
court may be resorted to, or someone as arbitrator.

If a benefic is simultaneously aspected or in the
7th House at birth, expect fair play and justice,
success in partnership, marriage or a court case.
If at the same time Neptune is badly aspected the
forecast involves fraud, chicanery, an alibi or a
proxy signature, double-dealing & misinformation.
If Saturn is involved there may be much time lost
because of a problem person or being too cautious.

The parallel of declination

Declination is a planet's distance above or below
the celestial equator (which is the earth's equator
projected out into space) and is north in the first
six Signs and south in the last six.   Two planets
within one degree of being the same in declination
are parallel, which is a magnetic aspect attracting
the two - we say that the thing is as good as done.

When the two planets are both in North Declination
or both in South Declination it operates like a conjunction of similar interests that attract and will
endure.   When one of the planets is in North Declination and the other South, it is like an opposition
of interests despite original attraction so that it
cannot endure and, like oppositions, must separate.

The parallel is nearly if not quite the strongest
aspect we have.   Certainly it is always dependably
decisive as an aspect confirming other aspects, and
should always be used.   It gives the minor planets
Venus and Mercury and the slow-moving malefics what
authority they need, and it also extends the vulnerable period for years in some instances (notably in
progressions involving the Sun and slower planets).
That is how long-standing marriages end in divorce.

Progressed & regressed planets

This writer finds that a forecast is emphasized in importance when a major aspect on a progressed date (so many days after birth) is confirmed by a strong aspect on the regressed date (that many days before birth, during the pre-natal period). The Regressed Moon is especially significant and should always be shown outside the wheel, to be activated during the year like the Progressed, Converse & Birthday Moons.

The progressed or regressed date on which a planet turns in direction either direct or retrograde will mark a turn in the native's affairs, usually noting the passing of someone in the circle or the loss of something such as a possession, money or employment, and a change in one's attitude or habits as regards the affairs and persons of the house where it turns. Mercury's turns involve us in an important decision whether made by ourselves or for us by someone else. Be sure to include this in your forecast that year.

A progressed or regressed planet changing Signs is indicative of a change in the temperament or habits which will be better or worse according to the planet's better or worse standing in the Sign it enters.

A progressed or regressed aspect to a planet retrograde at birth activates the tendency of such a condition to go-back-and-try-again, permitting a reconciliation during the year with someone of the house holding the natal planet. This may also forecast a return to some unfinished business or former haunt.

An aspect from one progressed planet to another is only noteworthy if the one being aspected is a slow-moving planet still close to its natal place & thus bounding an area between, whose midpoint will often time the aspect's culmination close to the forecast.

A progressed planet retrograding from aspecting an
angle or planet in the natal chart denotes less and
less interest in the matters of the house concerned
and in the person designated by the planet aspected.
If it were a malefic in bad aspect to the Ascendant
or its ruler or a planet in the 1st House, at birth
or by progression, it denotes conditions now easier
to handle, and personal bans or burdens now lifted.

Direct & Converse age-arcs

When only the year of the event is known, take the
age as the arc, otherwise use the Table on page 216.

Adding the age-arc moves the planets & the angular
cusps forward in the Signs (Direct Direction) while
subtracting the age-arc moves them backward, giving
their Converse Direction. They have equal power in
forecasting and in accounting for eventualities not
always shown by Secondary Progression, particularly
as regards the Arabian Points & slow-moving planets.

The Arabian Parts of Fortune, Marriage, Death, etc.
are directed by adding the age-arc and showing them
outside the wheel, then figuring their new solstice
points and showing them also.   The first office of
a solstice point is to attract your attention to an
upcoming TURNING-POINT in the affairs of the nature
of the Part it comes from, as part of your forecast.

Besides natal charts, those set for a horary question or for an event such as marriage or the filing
of a document can be directed by age-arc (time-arc)
to confirm a natal progression; as the death of the
querent in the chart on the opposite page set for a
horary question about lost-or-misplaced yardage but
also asking "What ELSE does it say?" which prompted
the astrologer to study Venus, ruler of the querent.
However, she was not given the disconcerting answer.

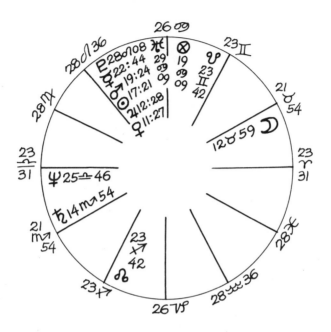

After investigating several time-arcs the concensus
was for 10 years after asking the question, or 1965
when the majority of aspects involved the death-8th.

VENUS the querent's ruler would in 10 years move to
21 Leo, square the death-8th cusp. The Moon, ruler
of the Fate-10th, would be 22 Taurus conjoining the
8th cusp. In a Scorpio decanate the Part of Fortune
is also the Part of Mis-fortune & in 10 years would
be 29:09 Cancer conjunct Uranus who rules the death-
8th House (this 5th) after the house holding VENUS.
The Part of Death moved to 12 Scorpio in opposition
to the Moon: the Ascendant conjoined the Part/Death.

See the querent's birth locality chart on page 204.
She died on March 13, 1965. Age-arc 70:40 directed
Uranus-ruler-8th to 18 Capri. opposition Ascendant,
& Saturn co-ruler 8th to 17 Sag. quincunx Ascendant.

How to proceed

With the natal chart before you, show the position
of the progressed Midheaven, Ascendant & planets in
red outside the wheel in order to quickly ascertain
their aspects to natal-planet symbols (also in red).
Show regressed planets if aspecting natal positions
in brackets - and always include the Regressed Moon
because any lunar presence in a house activates it,
even though it may have to wait there for a transit.
Any Moon if in an angular house affects the native
directly, aspecting or not; otherwise, other people.

Besides the Progressed Moon and Regressed Moon, we
also show the Directed Moon (add age-arc), Converse
Moon (subtract age-arc) and the Birthday Moon as on
the birthday each year in the current ephemeris. We
rely greatly on all these Moons because they always
account for most of the ACTIVITY during the period;
the Sun and planets are more significant of events.

Always mark with a small star ✳ any progressed or
regressed planet in a critical degree (as follows):

0-13-26 Cardinal Signs   9-21 Fixed   4-17 Common

They bring matters there to a head, so to say, during the coming year, forecasting a crisis or climax
in the matters of the house they are in. If in bad
aspect it will be unfavorably disruptive, but if in
good aspect matters will come to a favorable climax.
The month in which the Progressed Moon reaches such
a degree will prove to be especially worth watching.

Certain fixed stars have great upsetting influence
when conjunct natal or progressed planets or angles,
especially Caput Algol 24 Taurus, making the person
likely to "lose his head" - and the Weeping Sisters
(Pleiades) 29 Taurus giving something to weep about.

Planetary response and reaction

If the natal planet is a benefic or well aspected
to one at birth, or is well placed by Sign, angular
by house and not retrograde, it will respond easily
to the good aspects it receives.   The bad aspects
demand more effort in response & may entail a loss.

If the aspected planet is not well placed by Sign,
or is retrograde or in bad aspect at birth to a malefic, it reacts unfavorably and may go to extremes.

If the aspected planet is in an intercepted Sign &
early in degree and too slow-moving to ever get out
of the interception it may not be able to cooperate
or respond, so that the native does not participate.

If the aspected planet is in mutual reception with
another planet - each in the other's natural Sign -
which allows exchange status, it may not respond at
all but simply move off so that the aspect, good or
bad, goes unnoticed: the native does not take part.

If the natal planet is on both sides of the fence,
so to speak, by being simultaneously in good aspect
somewhere in the chart and also in bad aspect there
at birth, it will both respond & react accordingly,
with two different developments operating at once.

When transits are involved

A strong transit such as an eclipse can aspect any
planet whether natal, progressed or directed by age-
arc (which is the only way to appreciably move slow-
moving planets such as Uranus, Neptune, Pluto & Saturn).   An eclipse that is not visible at the birth-
place operates more as a strong lunation but is one
of the strongest activators we have and is also one
of the best indicators we have for timing an event.

Who is involved and how

First determine whether the main progressions are
either good or bad according to their favorable or
unfavorable aspects to the Ascendant, its ruler, or
a planet in any angular house of the chart at birth
and apply your reading to the native. If he is not
thus directly & personally affected, apply the reading to the matters & persons where the aspect falls.

In evaluating the following aspects, check back to
their basic meanings as given on pages 169 thru 171.

If by square, semisquare, sesquare, quincunx or opposition, expect a strenuous year with some loss or
bereavement, the necessity for readjustment and the
probability of having to take the blame for errors
of judgment. If by conjunction, affiliations will
be entered into or else broken off according to the
planet's direct or retrograde condition, especially
if it is Uranus or Mars. If it is Saturn-direct it
activates a long-pending matter in the house shown;
if he is retrograde, some matter of the house he is
in goes wrong, changes or dies out. If the aspect
is to Mercury, expect much coming-&-going and minor
annoyances, messages delayed or incorrect, and difficulties with relatives and affairs of that house.

If by trine, matters in the house involved proceed
easily & favorably; what is desired will be gained.
If the aspected planet is retrograde, the person is
advised to use his own judgment and work by himself.
If by sextile, an excellent opportunity for advancement will present itself - if the person accepts it,
which he may not do if the aspected planet is retrograde. If by quincunx, forecast a time of readjustment and reorganization in the affairs of the house
holding the aspected planet; if it is retrograde it
will be due to that person's illness or incapacity.

If by opposition, expect a separation of sorts during the year, lack of cooperation from the house in
which the aspected planet is found, an undercurrent
of envy or jealousy, & cessation of interest there.
The opposition also has to do with removals, and if
the progressed planet is in an angular house it can
mean a change of address. If in aspect to the Part
of Death (which includes Danger and Disaster) there
may be such a reason for the separation or removal.

Anything in the natal chart or by progression that
holds the same degree as the nodes & is included in
a progressed or directed aspect signifies trouble &
illness or an injury, casualty or fatality that may
affect the native only indirectly - others more so.
The progressed Moon is notably sensitive to aspects
to her nodes in this respect. An angular cusp conjunct a node itself at birth discloses a tragedy in
the life: by progression, expect it during the year.

Any aspect to Jupiter, Venus, the Part of Fortune,
the ruler of the 2nd House or a planet there brings
good luck and increase during the year. Show their
solstice points outside the wheel because they also
respond, like their owners, to a progressed aspect.

Enter eclipses & lunations during the year outside
the wheel, allowing three years for the Sun & three
months for the Moon to be answerable to any aspects.
Their solstice points often respond more than they.
An eclipse's impact registers a repercussion of the
effect 3 months and also 6 months afterward, around
the date when the Sun in the current ephemeris will
square and then oppose his initial eclipse position.

Eclipses recur every 19 years and should not cause
undue apprehension on the part of the adult native,
seeing that he has successfully lived through them
before & weathered their percussion & repercussion.

Forecasting by Progressions

To or from the Ascendant
If good
The native's personal affairs will be activated, &
he will participate successfully in whatever occurs
by the aspect. He should expect either a new enterprise or a change in his accustomed routine and outlook, & if conjunct a malefic will either accept or
be relieved of a responsibility or burden according
to that malefic's direct or retrograde condition at
the time, and to his advantage. His decisions will
be good and may involve many 3rd, 5th, 9th and 11th
House matters since any good aspect to the 1st activates its good sextile and trine mundane relationships to those houses. His circumstances, health &
self-reliance will improve and he will gain by many
opportunities coming to him because of his efforts.
If the Moon, Venus or Mercury is the aspecting power it brings a woman or young person to the fore, &
possibility of interest in real estate or marriage.
If it is Jupiter, there will be an increase in finances by salary, trade, pension or legacy; esteem &
credit, honors, & achievement in the matters of the
house he rules or is in, & possibility of marriage.
If bad
The native's personal affairs or interests will be
unfavorably involved and there will be danger of an
illness or accident. He will be drawn into matters
or developments tied to the 4th, 7th or 10th Houses
(also the 6th and 8th), because a bad aspect to the
1st House activates its mundane house relationships
by square, opposition or quincunx, affecting home &
family members, spouse, illness & surgery or death.

There will be planets in some of the houses listed
as well as those actually aspected to be taken into
consideration. For their good or bad effect, refer
to them as listed separately on pages 182 thru 186.

Forecasting by Progression

To or from the Midheaven

A planet within 10° orb of conjunction to the 10th
cusp from the 9th-House side is given consideration
equalling that of the 10th House or a planet there.
If good
The reputation, credit, standing in the community,
career or occupation will be enhanced; the ambition
assumes solidity, because the native strives harder
toward that end & earns more, especially when there
is a planet in the voluntary-labor-6th or money-2nd
due to a good aspect to the 10th arousing its good
trine mundane relationship to those houses.   Being
an angular house, there will be favorable publicity
which will reflect advantageously on his family because good aspects in an angular house register for
good in the opposite house. If Jupiter is involved
the native may branch out in his vocational pursuit
during the period or gain preferment in employment.
If bad
There will be some reflection on the native's credit or honor, trouble with the powers that be, unfavorable publicity, and loss of position or lessening
of industry, because bad aspects to the 10th arouse
its bad square mundane relationships to the 1st and
7th Houses, worrying the family also due to the mundane opposition to the 4th House.   Saturn, Uranus &
Neptune angular at birth will injure the standing &
cause a fall from power now; Uranus especially will
promote a separation or divorce during this period.
Mars causes accidents and trouble with authorities.

If the planet now being afflicted by this progression is a benefic or is in mutual reception so that
it has "exchange status" the person will be able to
avoid trouble.   The Sun or Moon above the horizon
at birth or a benefic angular protects the native.

Forecasting by Progressions

To or from the Sun
If good
FORTUNATE developments, prosperity, a new start if
changing Signs; advancement, gain by investment and
dealings with influential men: honors, concessions,
privileges or more authority granted and success in
ventures now under way - probably through the house
holding the natal Sun or his Sign Leo. Matrimonial
or domestic affairs improve, possibility of a child
in the family; better health & favorable publicity.
If bad
UNFORTUNATE for health, causing constitutional afflictions, fevers or injury.   There will be discord
in the family, bereavement, unfavorable publicity &
discredit or demotion, loss by extravagance or by a
necessary but large expenditure or by demand to pay
a debt or meet a family obligation.   Environmental
developments causing unhappy decisions and changes,
reversals in routine, sometimes enmity or distrust.

To or from the Moon
If good
FORTUNATE changes & decisions now; gain thru women
& employees, family members, travel & new contacts;
popularity; favorable for real estate purchase, new
possessions, improvements in the home. Better conditions in general in health and at work. Marriage
or birth of a child possible, or employment at home.
If bad
UNFORTUNATE changes; family or marital discord and
trouble at work; loss of property, money or possessions; bereavement; functional disorders, & surgery
if Mars is aspected or aspecting; discredit through
bad publicity involving a relative if Saturn, Venus
or Mercury is the afflicting planet. If Uranus (by
age-arc), an unexpected and unfavorable development.
From Neptune, tearful and discouraged or depressed.

To Saturn
If good

FORTUNATE & shrewd planning now for later returns;
the native will be industrious in whatever is ruled
by the house Saturn is in, consolidating his gains.
Dealings with older people, activity in serious and
sensible subjects, gain through inheritance, trade,
real estate or building, thrift & invested savings;
through taking responsibility; using tact, caution,
diplomacy, self-discipline and patient waiting. An
important and far-reaching matter will develop now.
The native meets his obligations at a fair discount.

If bad

UNFORTUNATE period; penalties exacted for mistakes
made or errors of judgment; criticism & unfavorable
publicity; loss or damage in the house Saturn is in
and delays in general. A time of depression, worry
& fear, bereavement, expenditure of savings; health
problems involving chronic ills, dentistry, falls &
accidents. Injury from elders, enemies or by theft.

To Uranus
If good

FORTUNATE turn of events, unexpected windfalls and
success in a new field of endeavor or new approach;
favorable changes, sudden romance or new membership.
Unusual circumstances or developments, independence,
original ideas now formulating for personal freedom.
Heroic measures taken this year in large-scale way.

If bad

UNFORTUNATE and vexatious emergencies will arise &
there may be an accident or disaster or injury from
an unexpected source. Danger of unbonded relationships or memberships ending in bad publicity; there
will be a broken tie, separation or divorce, a form
of exile, death in the family or circle; an illness
difficult to cure; a sudden journey with no return.
Disorganized schedules, rebellion against authority
& tendency toward unconventional thought or action.

To Jupiter
If good
FORTUNATE expansion in professional, evangelistic, academic, legal or publishing field; credit, honor, favorable publicity; will broaden the knowledge and pass examinations, gain by charity, social security, pension, insurance or through the courts. A period of greater prosperity and security despite untoward developments possible elsewhere.   Improved health.
If bad
UNFORTUNATE changes, over-expansion; poor judgment or over-optimism bring loss by extravagance or waiting too long to take action. Unfavorable publicity, disappointment in travel, writings, examinations or court decisions. Self-indulgence leading to health problems, blood disorders or trouble in the part of the body ruled by the Sign Jupiter is in or opposes.

To Mars
If good
FORTUNATE for starting new enterprises, entering a new territory, accepting a challenge, taking a definite stand and having the courage of one's convictions, taking the offensive, winning debates & lawsuits, profiting by using dynamic energy, accepting aid from powerful allies, using more discretion and tact, and taking no chances that may lead to danger, accident or surgery. A period of personal success.
If bad
UNFORTUNATE resistance against authority & arguing over small matters, championing a lost cause, rashness, truancy, disobedience, misuse of weapons & of tools or machines. Danger of bankruptcy and litigation, fire, theft, accident, major surgery, acute illness, assault, beating, murder, suicide, arrest, bereavement in the circle. An angry, upset period. The native is precipitous in action & takes on more than he can handle; exhausts his energies, savings, and patience. Changes cause loss and destruction.

To Mercury
If good
FORTUNATE changes & decisions; clever ideas having
to do with circulation & communication as in teaching, writing, publishing and advertising. May pass
examinations, travel, visit relatives or neighbors;
act in another's place, collect money, obtain small
favors, use machines or vehicles more than before &
adopt or adapt new methods or learn new mannerisms.
Engagement possible and dealings with young people.
May have a change of address at home or at business.
If bad
UNFORTUNATE changes or decisions, many mistakes or
errors of judgment; fruitless trips, wasted motions
or much coming-&-going to no purpose. Trouble with
contracts, signatures, writings, promises retracted
and appointments not kept. Disputes with tradesmen,
servants, mate, family, neighbors, tenants & agents.
Danger of libel, gossip, tale-bearing, false accus-
ations & petty quarrels. Restless period; nervous,
uneasy, forgetful, awkward, indecisive and critical.
There may be accidents, sleeplessness, incoherence,
inability to concentrate, or liability to epidemics.

To Venus
If good
FORTUNATE journey, removal or new contacts at this
time; success in meeting the public, in marital and
legal or religious matters; honor & esteem, credit,
gifts, money, advancement; gain by peaceful out-of-
court settlement. Favorable decisions, social and
artistic activities, romance, birth of a child; and
improved health and appearance thru hygienic means.
If bad
UNFORTUNATE changes, lower income or rank; extravagance, waste, dissipation, self-indulgence, errors
of judgment, misdeeds, carelessness. Trouble with
the health, reputation, mother, mate or partner, or
because of laziness, poor hygiene, or thru a woman.

To Neptune
If good

FORTUNATE period with gain by following hunches or
intuition; brings activity in fields of artistic or
inspirational expression, photography & the motion-
picture, television or entertainment world. Favorable association with benevolent people or agencies
& gain through travel, lucky breaks, hidden sources,
mysterious or spiritual channels; expect surprising
development related to the house holding the aspecting planet, particularly Uranus directed by age-arc.
Ideal romance possible & may have visions or dreams.

If bad

UNFORTUNATE period, chaotic conditions now, danger
of deception, fraud, displacement by a rival, widowhood or divorce, notoriety, loss thru untrustworthy
or unscrupulous persons or agencies; bereavement in
the circle; danger of assault, blackmail, seduction;
subversive, clandestine or illicit attractions; may
become addicted to drugs or alcohol.   Upset health,
illusions & delusions, hysteria, stage-fright, comatose conditions, fainting, panic; trouble with eyes,
feet & imaginary illnesses; may be badly frightened.

To Pluto
If good

FORTUNATE seclusion for research work & out-of-the-
ordinary interests; will become identified with for-
eigners or members of a group at this time but from
a detached position and will discard non-essentials.

If bad

UNFORTUNATE period, confused and complicated, with
tendency to withdraw from life; eccentric behavior;
rebellious, radically opposed to routine. Dealings
with the police, underworld figures or street gangs.
Someone depended on will be absent or alienated, in
an institution, under arrest, or may have passed on.
No gain from contests, legacies or insurance. Poor
health, sickness attended by serious complications.

11:38:00 p.m. EST January 19th, 1902 ... 74-W, 41-N

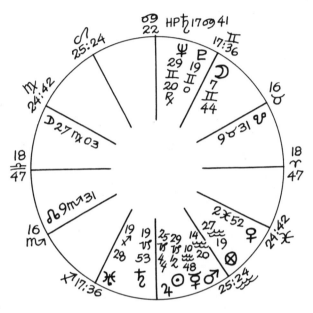

In 1941 the astrologer warned this woman of a great
loss in 1942 and again in 1948, probably by deaths;
first at age 40 when the directed Uranus would come
conjunct the Sun, representing the husband, & quincunx the widow-planet Neptune; while the progressed
Midheaven (end-of-marriage-4th for the marital 7th)
would exactly oppose Venus, her ruler. Her husband
died suddenly on Oct. 4, 1942 when the directed (D)
7 Scorpio was quincunx the Moon, a widow in the 8th.

Early in 1948, age-arc 45:20, Venus-ruler-Ascendant
in 18:12 Aries came to the 7th & she became engaged
but directed Mars-ruler-7th in 29 Pisces was square
Neptune-of-widows who also by direction was 14 Leo,
opposition Mars-ruler-7th. On June 20th, 1948, the
evening before the Full Moon 29 Sagittarius opposition Neptune, her fiancé died of a heart attack.

✳ ✳ ✳ ✳ ✳

D E L I N E A T I O N

o f

S P E C I A L   C H A R T S

ONE TOUCH OF WILL-POWER

Beauty unexpressed delights only the one in whose
hands it remains quiescent -- who alone appreciates
the loveliness of his jewel because he keeps others
from seeing it. Sometimes this is because the expression of a talent for painting, sculpture, writing and so on may require more opportunity or means
than the person possesses -- or he allows some illness or physical incapacity to frustrate his effort.

The plain and simple truth however is that "where
there is a will there is a way". For will-power in
the person there must be two things in his chart: a
square to the Ascendant or to a planet in the First
House to give him the will to do, and emphasis on a
Fixed Sign or decanate to assure fixity of purpose,
the staying-power to keep him on the beam so to say.
Squares have the dynamic power to push us onward, &
fixity establishes our purpose.   If the square to
the Ascendant is also in Fixed Signs the person cannot be turned aside; he knows early in life what he
wants to do and he does it sooner or later. If the
square is in Cardinal or Common Signs but there is
fixity elsewhere, he can be thwarted and frustrated
temporarily but he bides his time & succeeds later.

If the planet ruling the 10th House of the career
is retrograde it signifies delayed awareness of the
life work or delays in being able to return to what
was followed for awhile and put aside for a reason.
If intercepted the work is interfered-with until by
progression the planet changes Signs and leaves the
enclosing bars.   If the planet is in mutual reception (two planets in each other's natural Sign) the
person has two chosen careers he follows - and also
if the 10th or its ruler is in the dual Sign Gemini.

This is the natal chart of Pierre-Auguste Renoir, the artist recognized the world over as a master in the field of painting. He was born at 6:00 a.m. LMT on Feb. 25, 1841, at Limoges, France, 1E16 & 45N50.

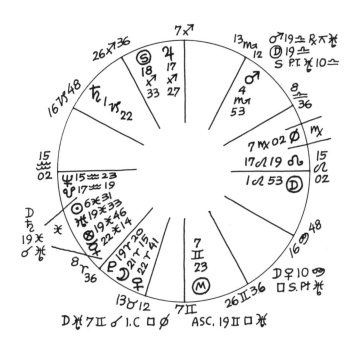

The first thing we notice is the presence of that much-desired square to the Ascendant from Mars & in Fixed Signs.   We say positively that here is a man of great persistence who will surely succeed in his aim and not be frustrated at any time by the interference shown by the interceptions in the 1st House.

Interceptions are formed by enclosing bars which have the same imprisoning effect as the barred 12th itself, a cadent house, so that the 3rd, 6th & 9th also tend to delay and hold in abeyance any planets

in these houses. It takes a square to the Ascendant
to overcome interference in the life, all the surer
if in Fixed Signs because they show determination &
the power to establish whatever plan they decide on.

The cause of this interference

The 1st House rules the native's health. The 6th
rules anything that can upset the health whether it
be physical, mental or emotional. If the ruler of
the Sign on the 6th cusp is in bad aspect with Sun,
Moon, ruler of the rising Sign or a malefic it will
affect the constitution (Sun) or functioning (Moon)
or part of the body ruled by the Sign the Ascendant-
ruler or malefic is in. If not a major bad aspect,
the native could learn to live with his affliction.

The interference here has to do with illness: the
Moon rules this 6th & is exactly semisquare the Sun
who is weak by Sign & still more by interception in
the physical 1st, so that there is a constitutional
malfunction. But we need at least three afflictions
involving the body before we can diagnose the sickness as serious: the other two here are the malefic
Saturn semisquare the Ascendant and the presence in
the 1st House of two malefics - Neptune and Uranus.
We also know that it was a very great disorder that
began at conception & established itself during the
9-month gestation period causing an abnormal health
condition at birth leading to some deformity later.

How do we know this? By Neptune conjunct either
the Moon or Ascendant in the natal chart, according
to this writer's simplified approach to recognizing
evidence at birth of prenatal malfunction resulting
in a congenital abnormality. This we read at once,
without having to know the prenatal month itself in
which the embryo underwent its abnormal development.

Thus we say that the Sign-and-degree positions of
the Moon and Ascendant in the natal chart are inter-
changed (taking each other's places) in setting the
chart for the time of conception and the charts for
the nine months more-or-less of the prenatal period.
For Renoir, all those charts thus had the Ascendant
in 21:15 Aries, and the Moon at each monthly return
approximately 15:02 Aquarius (her exact position in
the conception chart).   But the thing that we are
now interested in is simply that Neptune, who moves
hardly at all in a year's time, and is the abnormal
planet who lames, stunts and deforms, was always in
close conjunction with the Moon & thereby prevented
her functioning as the developer of a normal embryo.

Chronic-Saturn (rheumatism) semisquare the Ascendant; acute-&-inflammatory Mars (arthritis) squaring
the Ascendant; Uranus (paralysis) in the 1st square
Part of Sickness & Jupiter; & Neptune (abnormality)
conjunct the Ascendant all conspired against Renoir
physically.   He was crippled by rheumatic arthritis
and confined by paralysis to a wheel-chair for much
of his adult life.   Mars in the death-8th House and
elevated over both Sun & Moon gave acute arthritis
as the cause of death, so that we would expect Mars
to be active at the end of life, which was the case.

What the mutual reception reveals

One of the hidden revelations we find in reading
this chart is the mutual reception between Uranus &
Neptune which allows us to also read them as though
back in their own Sign but each in its same degree.
Neptune thus has a secondary place in 15:23 Pisces.

We find that around age 9 the Sun in 15:23 Pisces
would conjunct the mutual-reception Neptune and the
Moon-ruler-6th would be 15 Leo opposition Neptune &

the Ascendant, sesquare Saturn to set off his semisquare to Neptune at birth who was the cause of his
congenital infirmity in the first place.   This was
the time when Renoir's health impairment was first
recognized as a congenital affliction and it forced
him to withdraw from physical activity at that age.
As he reached the turning-point-age 13 his Sun progressed to conjunct the turning-point-planet Uranus
while his progressed Moon was conjunct Mars & semisquare the Part of Sickness 18 Sagittarius, so that
his illness became acute and more incapacitating, a
descriptive term for both malefics Uranus and Mars.

Age 13 also marked a turning-point in his life by
the simultaneous turning in direction of both Mars
and Mercury, the latter always coming to an important decision when changing direction.   This age-arc
13:00 directed Jupiter from the career-10th to conjunct Saturn-the-apprentice, and he began work as a
tyro painting miniatures on porcelain. (Neptune in
the 1st gave him an inborn talent for handling col-
or, love of porcelain & enamels, and a photographic
eye.)   His progressed Ascendant 6 Pisces conjoined
the Sun who himself had progressed to 19 Pisces conjunct Uranus who ruled the Ascendant and was receiving an exact square from the progressed career-10th,
the Midheaven in 19 Sagittarius which activated the
genius of Uranus always present when he is angular.
With such tremendous directions operating together,
especially at age 13, that first turning-point when
what we are to become in life gives its first hint,
it would have been strange indeed if Renoir had not
immediately launched himself on an artistic career.

As a painter, Renoir had his own original methods
of procedure and a special way of preparing his can-
vases and applying his pigments; and this is immediately apparent in his chart.   The Sign of originality is Aquarius, on his Ascendant & holding Neptune

the planet of painting, color sense, and unorthodox
procedure expressed in the highest degree by mutual
reception with Uranus whose keywords are inventive-
ness & originality. Also, his Moon's latitude 4:31
was very wide (being so close to 5:18 her greatest)
and such people are free from slavish conformity to
conventional methods. However, it is the square of
Mars to the Ascendant emphasized by the fixed qual-
ity of the Signs that is what kept him doggedly and
persistently at his easel all his life.   His tools
were his Mercury hands which were said to have been
noticeably small & delicate; nonetheless, the fixed
decanate 22 Pisces reveals that he had the strength
of Scorpio, the strongest Sign in the Zodiac "there
in the palm of his hand" so to say, though crippled
by conjunction to Uranus and square also to Jupiter.
Crippled hands, yes -- but weak, no. He turned out
a prodigious number of incalculably great paintings.

Additional disclosures

For the student seeking confirmation of what else
he reads, Renoir's father was a shoemaker, as shown
by the father-4th ruled by Mercury-of-hands in foot-
wear-Pisces in the father's occupation-10th - which
is this 1st - conjunct its ruler Uranus in the same
Sign. His workshop was in the home, as seen by the
ruler of his 10th, Uranus, in an angular house (the
home) and squeezed-in within rooms by interception.

Jupiter in-and-ruling the mother-10th and sextile
spiritual Neptune explains her deeply religious and
benevolent nature, confirmed by the mother-Moon and
Jupiter in close trine. She was a very pretty woman
fond of social life as shown by Moon conjunct Venus.

Renoir himself was of very high spiritual & moral
caliber, what with Jupiter high in the chart, sext-

ile Neptune in the lst House and trine the Moon who
rules his 6th House of habits. Mars sextile Saturn
gives moral strength, trine the Sun gives religious
leanings especially in Pisces who accepts on faith.
His was an exceptionally happy marriage, always the
case with benefic Jupiter trine Venus from the 10th
(end-of-the-matter-4th House after the marital-7th,
showing how the marriage will turn out). And it is
true that she did the proposing, what with the Sun,
ruler of the 7th, coming over to his house; particularly when trine the impulsive Mars & conjunct the
romantic Uranus. He was left a widower, as seen by
the Star of Widowhood Vindemiatrix in 8:41 Libra on
the death-8th and on 7:46 Libra, the solstice point
of Mercury co-ruler of the wife-7th to indicate her.
The Part of Marriage 7 Gemini squaring the sinister
Lilith in the marriage-7th has the same fatal power.

Applying Wynn's #14 Theory to this chart

The number of the house in which a planet appears
is subtracted from 14, the remainder being the number of another house where the planet's effect will
be strongly felt.   Renoir's Saturn in the 11th of
circumstances over which he had little control left
his schooling up to him because it operated in the
3rd (14 - 11 = 3) where he was self-taught to great
extent; an advantage when the child knows more than
those who would teach him their way & spoil genius.

Apply this method to your own charts for additional insight in reading them. Planets in the lst and
7th Houses do not change (14 - 1 = 13 - 12 = 1, and
14 - 7 = 7) so that one's personal affairs & those
of others with whom he deals will remain personal.

The benefic Jupiter in Renoir's 10th not only protected his reputation but also blessed his family &

his home (14 - 10 = 4th) and his was a happy family.
Mars in the 8th of any form of taxation squared his
Ascendant and taxed his strength by the natural in-
clination of Mars to over-work, which registered in
the illness-6th (14 - 8 = 6) causing his breakdowns.

The death of Renoir

On December 3rd, 1919 Renoir breathed his last as
his progressed Ascendant 19 Gemini squared his ruler Uranus, while progressed Mars 19R Libra together
with the directional Part of Death also in 19 Libra
in the death-8th were quincunx to Uranus (the death
aspect).   On that day, transiting Mars 1:22 Libra
squared Saturn 1:22 Capricorn in the 11th, and made
death part of the existing circumstances. While it
is true that transiting Mars had done this often in
Renoir's life, never before was progressed Mars accompanied by the directed Part of Death, afflicting
Uranus in the 1st House, both progressed & transiting Mars working against him at one & the same time.

We should always be careful not to be dismayed by
transiting malefics whose progressed or directional
places at birth are not also evilly disposed. Such
ordinary transits come from outside the chart: they
represent outsiders or ordinary influence coming in
for temporary activity according to their duration.

Using the directional age-arc

At his death, Renoir was 78 years, 9 months and 8
days old, which the list of Major Arcs gives as age
arc 77:38. Adding this to all the planets & points
in the chart at birth gives their directed places,
particularly valuable as regards the slower planets
that otherwise move so slowly, relatively speaking,

that they may never register at all by progression.
Also, using the age-arc is the only way to progress
the Arabian Points: thus the Part of Death 1:53 Leo
was directed to 19 Libra to operate with progressed
Mars 19R Libra by the death-aspect quincunx Uranus,
Renoir's physical significator in-&-ruling the 1st.

Being in the hylegiacal 1st House, the Sun is the
Giver of Life for Renoir, always menaced by Lilith,
the death-dealing power exactly square the end-of-
life-4th but delayed by interception until the ruler of the Ascendant Uranus reached there to end the
matter.   By the age-arc 77:38, the directed Uranus
in 7 Gemini exactly conjoined the 4th cusp, squared
Lilith & activated her threat to his Giver of Life.

The directed Mars 22 Capricorn squared Venus rul-
er death-8th: Venus herself in 10 Cancer was square
Uranus' solstice point 10 Libra in the death-8th, &
Saturn-the-Reaper in 19 Pisces was exactly conjunct
Uranus & the Part of Misfortune in the physical-1st.
Forecasting death requires several such testimonies.

What makes a life significant?

A badly-afflicted chart puts difficulties in life
that deny good health or a good education or assistance when needed, but the very aspects that afflict
the chart contain within themselves the power necessary to overcome their impact & make our lives significant thru will-power. Squares give will-power &
self-application: oppositions grant time for growth
and the practice needed to perfect ourselves in our
chosen field.   Significance in life is revealed by
progressions or directions operating simultaneously
& in number, as in Renoir's experience, designating
our high-lights in life -- including our departure.

☆ ☆ ☆ ☆ ☆

THE MOON AND THE OVERWEIGHT PROBLEM

People whose natal Moon is moving away from the Sun so that she is increasing in light & so getting bigger, are more prone to obesity because she rules physical development and has been empowered by conjunction to the Sun, ruler of growth, to enlarge in size to her limit which is her Full Moon or obesity phase. For several days before and after the conjunction she is crescent; her ideally slender form, though human beauty requires a little more padding.

The Moon has four phases or quarters. Her conjunction to the Sun marks her New Moon period which is her 1st quarter lasting seven days, during which she increases in size until she squares the Sun and this generally describes the adult as well-rounded. From being well-rounded, her 2nd quarter of another seven days increases to her Full Moon period opposition the Sun, describing the adult as quite plump. In her 3rd quarter of seven days she leaves obesity because she is decreasing in light (weight), and by the time she again squares the Sun at the beginning of her last quarter she describes the adult as well-rounded, as before. In her last quarter, moving to conjunct the Sun, thus losing in size, the adult is described as well-rounded inclining to slenderness. From the effects of the Moon's quarters we can know the native's approximate weight and if reduction is required we take action during her decreasing phase.

People come in assorted sizes and shapes due to the assorted aspects possible between Moon and Sun. Besides the conjunction, square and opposition, she can be intermediate in aspect and thus intermediate in size by being semisextile, semisquare, sextile, trine, sesquare, or quincunx the Sun, registering a little more or a little less in weight accordingly.

The size of an increasing Moon at birth is also
subject to modification if in bad aspect with limiting Saturn, energetic Mars, contradictory Uranus or
illusive Neptune; or the physical Ascendant, making
for fluctuation in weight from time to time.   This
is more apparent when she is within 3 or 4 days' motion past the conjunction of the Sun, still thinned
but gaining slowly and lacking in her expected size.

The natal Moon having left the Sun's opposition
is decreasing in light; a reduction in size that in
the native is reflected in a reduction in weight, &
especially in her last quarter.   For an overweight
problem, then, we not only give particular consideration to the Moon when increasing at birth but also
when increasing by progression (and by transit when
the overweight native is under reducing treatment).

When a too-heavy person goes on a reducing diet
& exercise regimen, which he should for a diversity
of reasons such as better health and longer life as
well as freedom from self-consciousness when among
other people, he should remember that each phase of
the Moon covers seven days and thus he should start
with the Full Moon and lose in size along with her.
Logically, he should be able to do this appreciably
by the next New Moon two weeks away, but it depends
on how much weight can be lost safely.   If the progressed Moon is increasing in light the native will
want to eat more, so that any dietary lapse counteracts a transiting-decreasing Moon's reducing power.

If only somewhat overweight, start with the 1st
quarter New Moon on a 3½-day liquid diet (fruit and
vegetable juices, coffee and tea taken plain, soups
& skim milk), augmented during the next 3½ days of
this quarter by green salads, vegetables, red meat,
fish, whole-wheat products, etc., omitting sauces &
dressings, starches, sweets & all fattening fruits.

This non-fat diet supplies the minerals, vitamins &
bulk the body needs but not the extra calories that
it doesn't need, so that it draws on its own store.
If the few extra pounds are then lost, follow a non-
fat diet thereafter. Brisk walks, outdoor work and
games will quicken the losing pace but retain tone.

So much for ordinary reduction to keep in trim.
If obese, however, stay on this regimen for as many
months as necessary, starting every Full Moon phase
with the first 3½ days' liquid diet as already sug-
gested. Rapid reducing of obese cases is extremely
undesirable and even dangerous, however, because of
too-radical a change in the established tempo (seeing that most cases of obesity involve Leo and thus
the heart, the body's motor). It is safer to make
haste slowly, so more leeway in diet is allowed, to
include whole milk, eggs, potatoes, etc. during the
tapering-off period of months - even a year in some
cases, especially if Leo is prominent in the chart.

The Moon increasing in light

If the Moon at birth is increasing in light and
in any Fixed Sign (Taurus, Leo, Scorpio & Aquarius)
she adds girth: also in a Venus or Jupiter Sign, or
in bad aspect to (or conjunct) these plump planets.
In Water Signs the girth is subject to modification
by fluctuation, these being tidal with a propensity
to ebb & flow, causing irregular changes in weight.

The Moon decreasing in light

If the Moon at birth is decreasing in light the
native does not tend to become overweight in adult-
hood. The nearer the Moon is to the Sun during her
first and last quarters, the more slender the adult
as a rule; and if conjunct the Sun the adult verges
on thinness similar to the Moon's slender crescent.

This is the chart of a woman whose birthtime is
unknown so we use what is the best substitute for a
regular chart, a Johndro Birth LOCALITY Chart using
Right Ascension instead of Sidereal Time, & set for
her birth locality 88W27 42N19 & date May 20, 1893.

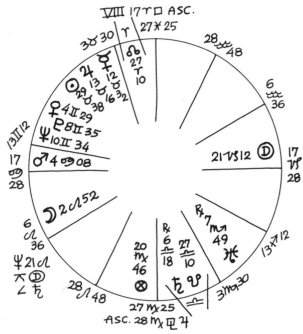

This woman was plump from birth, as seen by the
Moon increasing in light in the physical 1st House,
in the danger-of-obesity Sign Leo square to Jupiter
who rules her nourishment-6th & is in the nutriment
Virgo decanate of Taurus - who can be a heavy eater
in the 11th, the house ruling circumstances in life
that can get out of control. She became a compulsive eater and weighed over 330 pounds when she died
on March 13, 1965 of a number of ailments: kidney &
bladder malfunction (Mars square Saturn in Libra, &
Moon square Uranus in Scorpio) as well as fatty de-
generation of the heart (Moon afflicted in Leo) and
a major stroke when her age-arc 70:47 directed the

Ascendant to 28 Virgo conjunct the end-of-life-4th.
Its exact sesquare to Jupiter denied saving grace &
thus nullified the Ascendant-trine-Sun in 29 Taurus
the apoplexy part of the brain ill-starred by being
conjunct the unfortunate Pleiades. In passing, let
us note how precisely the Johndro cusps operate and
particularly this directed Ascendant. The directed
death-8th cusp 17 Aries exactly squared the Ascendant itself; Uranus-ruler-8th then 8 Capricorn moved
to quincunx Pluto (8th-house aspect) & she suffered
sudden & complete physical paralysis and died peace-
fully in her sleep as comatose-Neptune 21 Leo moved
to the exact quincunx of the Part of Death 21 Capricorn & to the semisquare of Saturn in the grave-4th.

The compulsion to eat

There are many kinds of hungers besides the one
that is normal to the body for its replenishment or
natural growth, and many hungers have nothing to do
with appetite per se. Denial, frustration or other
emotional maladjustments often drive people to find
solace in eating which appeases and thus silences,
at least for a time, the sufferer's emotional pangs.

The cause of this woman's compulsion to eat was
unceasing resentment over marital estrangement (but
not separation) dating back to 1920 when Saturn the
ruler of the marriage-7th moved by age-arc 26:32 to
2:50 Scorpio square the Moon ruler of the Ascendant
while the Moon 29 Leo squared the Sun. The Part of
Fortune thus in 17:18 Libra squared the marital-7th
but in the 4th & they were strangers under one roof.
The Sun & Moon in Fixed Signs do not forgive easily.

Natal Mars badly placed by Sign & house, square
Saturn-ruler-7th in the home-4th means domestic in-
harmony. Saturn retrograde in the 4th brings coldness in the family. Estrangement is shown by Nept-

une's solstice point 19 Cancer conjunct the Ascendant and thus opposition the marital-7th. But there
would be no divorce because the divorce planet Uranus is not in the 7th or 10th: not even his solstice
point 22 Aquarius, which would also denote divorce.

When the cause is not emotional

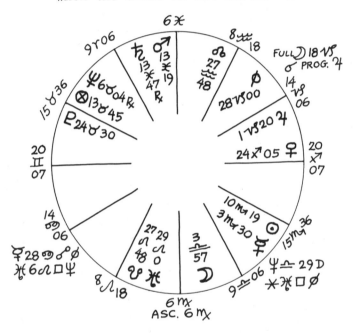

This is the natal chart of the Aga Khan III who
was otherwise His Highness the Sultan Mahomed Shah,
born in Karachi, India, 67E02 24N52 at 7:45:00 p.m.
LMT November 2, 1877, the 44th lineal descendant of
the Prophet Mahomet thru his daughter Fatima. His
wealth was as enormous as his weight which was measured out to him in gold every year by his subjects.
Although of only average height, he weighed 240 lbs
and could have been heavier if the Moon had been increasing in light at his birth.   In a Venus-ruled
Sign, however, the Moon would still show overweight

because of her bad aspect to Jupiter, lover of wine
and the good things of life to excess, adding still
more to Jupiter's self-indulgence by his mutual application to the trine of Neptune in gourmet-Taurus
in the 11th House where eating is likely to get out
of hand, so to speak, by Neptune reaching across to
Mercury his Ascendant-ruler in the 5th of pleasures
and especially banquets: and he would have many opportunities for these with Mercury sextile Jupiter.

The 6th House rules both habits and ill-health,
so that habits can cause ill-health that can become
habitual. This is the answer to the Sultan's overweight problem. The ruler of his 6th, Pluto, is in
overeating Taurus and ill-starred by exact conjunction to Caput Algol the headless Medusa, describing
one who in the 12th House of self-undoing habitual-
ly loses his head in the dining-room and gains more
weight than his heart can cope with, because square
to the irresponsible Uranus in the danger-Sign Leo.

Being warned to diet, he went to extremes, losing weight too rapidly; going down to 120 pounds in
too short a time for the long-established tempo his
heart was adjusted to, and it failed. At age 79 he
died of a heart attack on July 11, 1957, the day of
the Full Moon in 18 Capricorn exactly conjunct progressed Jupiter in the death-8th; while transiting-
Neptune that day turned Direct in 29 Libra, sextile
Uranus in Leo & square Lilith the malefic dark moon
of death in the 8th; timed by opposition from transiting Mercury, Ascendant-ruler, in 28 Cancer. Uranus by transit in 6 Leo squared Neptune-ruler-10th -
and his high position in life came to a sudden halt.

His regular progressions were mainly cuspal, as
the Ascendant conjoined the end-of-life-4th - where
the Moon was receiving the opposition of progressed
death-8th in 3 Aries, quincunx to his ruler Mercury.

＊ ＊ ＊ ＊ ＊

Mischa Auer, St. Petersburg, Russia (now Leningrad)

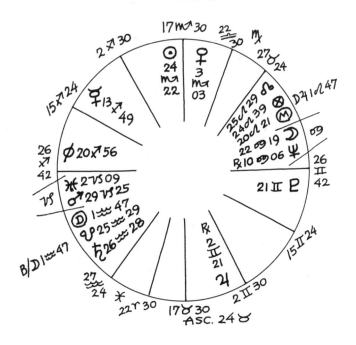

Parallels of..Mercury 24S54..Declination
            Uranus   23S41
            Ascend: 23S25
            Neptune 22N06
            Mars   21S51
            Jupiter 19N39
            Sun   18S54
            Moon   18N50
            M.C.   17S03
            Saturn   14S12
            Fortuna 13N20
            Venus   11S10

11:17:00 a.m. LMT, November 17, 1905, 30E15 59N55
15:39:33 S.T. 16th 15:00:05 Calc S.T. 2:01 EGMT
9:16 a.m. GMT Nov. 17th = 9435 Constant Logarithm

MR. OUNSKOWSKI'S REMARKABLE BIRTHDAY MOON

The Moon being the handmaid of the earth on which
we live & temporarily have our being, starts us off
each year on our birthday anniversary by disclosing
her intended activity in the ensuing twelve months
according to the aspect she makes from the position
she is in by transit in the current ephemeris.   It
is the strongest activity-transit we can have based
on her power to effect CHANGES in life's status quo
and she thus FORECASTS the development most important to the native in the forthcoming year's period.

On the opposite page is presented the natal chart
for Mischa (Ounskowski) Auer, famous actor-comedian
whose rise in life from adversity would be certain,
as shown by the Sun in the 10th sextile Mars-ruler-
10th, parallel Jupiter-ruler-Ascendant, & trined by
the Moon in her own Sign & also in an angular house.
From the arrangement of parallels of declination we
recognize the ladder he had to climb in life, their
steady continuity taking him steadily up to the top.

This writer rectified the birth hour by the first
major event as usual, which in this case was at age
three when the father died in mid-1908 & before the
native's birthday late in the year (in November) so
that the 1907 ephemeris was used to find the Birthday Moon.   It was in 3 Taurus, parallel-opposition
Venus ruler of the father-4th House denoting a separation of one sort or another between them during
the year.   That it would be by death was indicated
by progressed Mars 1:45 Aquarius conjunct the Part
of Death 1:47 Aquarius, by progressed Sun-ruler-8th
(death) square Saturn (natural ruler of the father)
and by the Part of Fortune directed by age-arc 3 to

the opposition of Saturn from the father's end-of-
life-4th (this 7th). As a rule, the events in this
man's life occurred before his birthday so that the
preceding year's ephemeris is used as in this case.

At age 12 & during the Russian Revolution, he was
sent to Siberia along with other children of the
intelligentsia. Ragged children they were, to whom
staying alive meant begging & stealing on one's own.
His Birthday Moon 26 Leo was opposition Saturn, who
in the 1st House throws the native on his own early
in life, usually because of the father's misfortune
or loss.   But planets in mutual reception give exchange status enabling the native to free himself &
get out of or rise above misfortune or frustration,
& this chart gives double indemnity in that respect
through Saturn-M/R-Uranus and Mercury-M/R-Jupiter.
Thus in 1918 before his birthday he and his mother
were reunited & were able to escape. They attached
themselves to the British Expeditionary Forces, and
his mother established a refugee hospital, while he
at 13 became an ambulance driver.   She died there
during a typhus epidemic, although the date is not
now available, but his Birthday Moon in 2 Capricorn
still conjoined Uranus & was quincunx his ruler Jupiter in the family-4th for the loss.   It was also
still sextile Venus-of-jewels in the travel-9th and
he sold his mother's jewels to pay his way to Italy
where he lived with her friends until age 15 (1920).

In 1920 his mother's father, Leopold Auer, world-
renowned violinist then living in America, not only
gave him transportation to America to live with him
but his name Auer as well in lieu of the cumbersome
Ounskowski.   His Birthday Moon in 10 Libra squared
Neptune in Cancer for the voyage and then sextiled
Mercury who rules names, is in the 11th-of-adoption
and changing circumstances, and in mutual reception
with Jupiter, his Ascendant ruler, for the new name.

His first marriage ended in divorce early in 1941, his Birthday Moon 2 Cancer opposition divorce-Uranus. In that same year but after his birthday he married again: his Birthday Moon 3 Scorpio was then conjunct Venus in the ritual-9th.   At his third marriage in 1950 the Birthday Moon 22 Libra was conjunct the 9th cusp but square the Moon in the matrimonial 7th, and it ended in divorce in 1957, the Birthday Moon being 17 Taurus exactly conjunct the end-of-the-matter-4th and exactly sesquare the divorce planet Uranus.   At his fourth marriage Sept. 22, 1965 his Birthday Moon 3 Taurus was parallel-opposition Venus in the ritual 9th, while his age-arc 58°59' moved the Part of Marriage from 20:21 Leo to 19:20 Libra with only a few years to last before squaring the Moon in the marital 7th, and it ended on March 5, 1967 when he died.

Remarkably enough, his final Birthday Moon in 1:47 Aquarius was exactly conjunct the Part of Death 1:47 Aquarius and square Venus ruling his end-of-life-4th while progressed Ascendant 24 Taurus was exactly conjunct the malefic fixed star Caput Algol, opposition the Sun ruling his death-8th, and unfortunate by exact square to the Part of Fortune in the heart Sign Leo, and he died of a heart attack.   His heart would cause concern at both birth and death because he had the Leo decanate on the Ascendant and Leo on the 8th cusp itself, therefore we direct his Ascendant-ruler Jupiter by adding his age-arc 59°26' which moved him astonishingly to 1:47 Leo-the-heart exactly opposite the Part of Death and also the Birthday Moon there.

This work with the Birthday Moon was originated by this writer and its infallibility confirmed by diligent research and a great number of authentic charts. Students will find the method exceedingly simple and moreover valuable in rectification of the birth time.

✴ ✴ ✴ ✴ ✴

CYCLES and YEARS

In his "Practical Astrology" St Germain lists these
cycles & years from 1801 to 1938. We figured them
through 2052, however, and explain their uses here.
The CYCLES contain 36 years each & are ruled by the
days of the week in reverse order. The planets ruling the YEARS follow a unique order: Venus, Mercury,
Moon, Saturn, Jupiter, Mars, Sun. The planet ruling
the Cycle rules both its first year & its last year.
The nature of the planet ruling your Cycle is part
of your nature for life and you will express it according to the nature of the one ruling your year.

VENUS CYCLE, 1801-1836
36 years inclusive

```
VENUS - - 1801, 1808, 1815, 1822, 1829, 1836
Mercury - 1802, 1809, 1816, 1823, 1830
Moon  - - 1803, 1810, 1817, 1824, 1831
Saturn  - 1804, 1811, 1818, 1825, 1832
Jupiter - 1805, 1812, 1819, 1826, 1833
Mars  - - 1806, 1813, 1820, 1827, 1834
Sun - - - 1807, 1814, 1821, 1838, 1835
```

JUPITER CYCLE, 1837-1872

```
JUPITER - 1837, 1844, 1851, 1858, 1865, 1872
Mars  - - 1838, 1845, 1852, 1859, 1866
Sun - - - 1839, 1846, 1853, 1860, 1867
Venus - - 1840, 1847, 1854, 1861, 1868
Mercury - 1841, 1848, 1855, 1862, 1869
Moon  - - 1842, 1849, 1856, 1863, 1870
Saturn  - 1843, 1850, 1857, 1864, 1871
```

MERCURY CYCLE, 1873-1908

```
MERCURY - 1873, 1880, 1887, 1894, 1901, 1908
Moon  - - 1874, 1881, 1888, 1895, 1902
Saturn  - 1875, 1882, 1889, 1896, 1903
Jupiter - 1876, 1883, 1890, 1897, 1904
Mars  - - 1877, 1884, 1891, 1898, 1905
Sun - - - 1878, 1885, 1892, 1899, 1906
Venus - - 1879, 1886, 1893, 1900, 1907
```

As time goes on, you enter new Cycles that indicate
by the new ruler a particular planet to consider in
your natal chart, noting also the house it is in at
birth. You also note the planet ruling the current
year and the natal house it is in. These will have
a bearing on the developments & events of the year.

MARS CYCLE, 1909-1944
```
MARS  - - 1909, 1916, 1923, 1930, 1937, 1944
Sun - - - 1910, 1917, 1924, 1931, 1938
Venus - - 1911, 1918, 1925, 1932, 1939
Mercury - 1912, 1919, 1926, 1933, 1940
Moon  - - 1913, 1920, 1927, 1934, 1941
Saturn  - 1914, 1921, 1928, 1935, 1942
Jupiter - 1915, 1922, 1929, 1936, 1943
```
MOON CYCLE, 1945-1980
```
MOON  - - 1945, 1952, 1959, 1966, 1973, 1980
Saturn  - 1946, 1953, 1960, 1967, 1974
Jupiter - 1947, 1954, 1961, 1968, 1975
Mars  - - 1948, 1955, 1962, 1969, 1976
Sun - - - 1949, 1956, 1963, 1970, 1977
Venus - - 1950, 1957, 1964, 1971, 1978
Mercury - 1951, 1958, 1965, 1972, 1979
```
S U N CYCLE, 1981-2016
```
SUN - - - 1981, 1988, 1995, 2002, 2009, 2016
Venus - - 1982, 1989, 1996, 2003, 2010
Mercury - 1983, 1990, 1997, 2004, 2011
Moon  - - 1984, 1991, 1998, 2005, 2012
Saturn  - 1985, 1992, 1999, 2006, 2013
Jupiter - 1986, 1993, 2000, 2007, 2014
Mars  - - 1987, 1994, 2001, 2008, 2015
```
SATURN CYCLE, 2017-2052
```
SATURN  - 2017, 2024, 2031, 2038, 2045, 2052
Jupiter - 2018, 2025, 2032, 2039, 2046
Mars  - - 2019, 2026, 2033, 2040, 2047
Sun - - - 2020, 2027, 2034, 2041, 2048
Venus - - 2021, 2028, 2035, 2042, 2049
Mercury - 2022, 2029, 2036, 2043, 2050
Moon  - - 2023, 2030, 2037, 2044, 2051
```

* * * * *

T E R M I N O L O G Y

as used in this book

The reference books named herein

are listed on the copyright page.

TABLE of MAJOR ARCS

Age	Arc	Age	Arc	Age	Arc	Age	Arc
1	0:59	26	25:38	51	50:16	76	74:55
2	1:58	27	26:37	52	51:15	77	75:54
3	2:57	28	27:36	53	52:14	78	76:53
4	3:57	29	28:35	54	53:13	79	77:52
5	4:56	30	29:34	55	54:13	80	78:51
6	5:55	31	30:33	56	55:12	81	79:50
7	6:54	32	31:32	57	56:11	82	80:49
8	7:53	33	32:32	58	57:10	83	81:49
9	8:52	34	33:31	59	58:09	84	82:48
10	9:51	35	34:30	60	59:08	85	83:47
11	10:51	36	35:29	61	60:07	86	84:46
12	11:50	37	36:28	62	61:07	87	85:45
13	12:49	38	37:27	63	62:06	88	86:44
14	13:48	39	38:26	64	63:05	89	87:43
15	14:47	40	39:26	65	64:04	90	88:42
16	15:46	41	40:25	66	65:03	91	89:42
17	16:45	42	41:24	67	66:02	92	90:41
18	17:44	43	42:23	68	67:01	93	91:40
19	18:44	44	43:22	69	68:01	94	92:39
20	19:43	45	44:21	70	69:00	95	93:38
21	20:42	46	45:20	71	69:59	96	94:37
22	21:41	47	46:20	72	70:58	97	95:36
23	22:40	48	47:19	73	71:57	98	96:36
24	23:39	49	48:18	74	72:56	99	97:35
25	24:38	50	49:17	75	73:55	100	98:34

Mos--Arc		Mos--Arc		Mos--Arc		Days		Arc
						4 thru 9		1'
1	5'	5	25'	9	44'	10 " 15		2'
2	10'	6	30'	10	49'	16 " 21		3'
3	15'	7	34'	11	54'	22 " 27		4'
4	20'	8	39'	12	59'	28 & over		5'

TERMINOLOGY

For brevity, include the Sun & Moon as planets

AFFLICTION: The harmful effect on the Ascendant or any planet when square, semisquare, sesquare or conjunct a malefic planet or if alone between Mars and Saturn (besieged) no matter how far apart. In the First House, a malefic afflicts the health of the native & the well-being of a horary question.

ANGLES, ANGULAR: The 1st, 4th, 7th & 10th cusps are the angles of the chart; they mark the angular houses. Angular planets are those in these houses.

APPLICATION: The forward "applying" movement of a faster planet aspecting a slower one that is direct. If the slower one is retrograde, they face each other in MUTUAL APPLICATION to their aspect.

ARC: Any part of a circle. **ARC OF DIRECTION:** the degrees required for a planet or cusp to complete an aspect; the degrees are also the AGE-ARC.

ASCENDANT: The cusp of the First House. In the older books it is also called the Horoscope but we of today use that name for the entire natal chart.

ASPECT: To look at (the ancients said "behold") A mathematical relationship as in the aspects conjunction within 8° apart, sextile 60°, square 90°, trine 120°, sesquare 135°, quincunx 150°, & opposition 180°. For the parallel, within 1° of being the same in declination; both may be North or both South declination, operating like a conjunction to endure. If one is North declination and the other South, the parallel separates like an opposition.

BENEFIC: The good aspects: conjunction when not to a malefic; sextile, trine and parallel.   The BENEFICS are Jupiter the Greater Benefic and Venus the Lesser Benefic, still more so if not afflicted.

BESIEGED: Between evil forces, as a planet between Mars & Saturn, no matter how far apart.   The closer the three, the worse the effect of duress.

CADENT: Falling (behind angular houses). These are the 3rd, 6th, 9th and 12th Houses; and because they are between a private-succeedent and public-angular house they represent whatever is semi-public-&-semi-private such as prayers said in church, secrets told in letters, private life in the news.

CARDINAL SIGNS: Cancer-North, Aries-East, Libra-West and Capricorn-South, designating the cardinal points N.E.W.S.   Taken in that order, they bring world NEWS in Ingress Charts for city or country.

CELESTIAL EQUATOR: The earth's equator extended out into space (the heavens or Celestial Sphere).

COLLECTION OF LIGHT: In a horary chart, a third planet receiving an aspect from two planets never in aspect to each other (strangers). It signifies that two strangers can meet by applying to a third person, as a real-estate agent or marriage broker.

COMMANDING SIGNS: The first six lead & command others & their own fate: the last six follow, obey & bow to their fate. It reveals much in marriage.

COMMON SIGNS: Gemini, Virgo, Sagittarius & Pisces. A better term is MUTABLE or ADAPTABLE Signs because they can adapt themselves to the fixity of Fixed Signs plus the movability of Cardinal Signs, between which they are placed and have to balance.

CONFIGURATION: Planetary arrangement by aspect, as the Moon in Aries trine Venus in Leo. If both aspected Mars in Aquarius (Moon sextile and Venus opposition) they would be in a mixed configuration showing both favorable and unfavorable conditions.

CONSTELLATIONS: Groups of fixed stars named for the Ram, the Bull, the Twins, the Crab, the Lion, the Virgin, the Scales, the Scorpion, the Archer, the Goat, the Pitcher-bearer diffusing the ethers, & the Fishes. They formerly fell irregularly near the 12 Signs (30-degree sections of the 360-degree circle) & were identified with them but no longer.

CONVERSE DIRECTION: To move a planet or a cusp backward by subtracting the Arc of Direction; when we add the Arc we have DIRECT DIRECTION. See page 54 of "Foundation of the Astrological Chart", illustrating its importance with the slower planets.

CONVERTIBLE: Subject to change: said of Mercury who rules mercury (quicksilver used in mirrors and thus reflective of whatever it faces). Mercury's nature reflects that of the planet he most closely aspects. The native's mental faculties reflect the masculine or feminine manner of expression according to the sex of the Sign Mercury is in at birth.

CRITICAL DEGREES: These are degrees that emphasize the planets or angles they conjunct. They are derived from the Moon's average daily motion 13:11 degrees through the Signs, starting at 0-Aries as:

0-13-26 of Cardinal Signs: 9-21 Fixed: 4-17 Common

Natal planets or angles in critical degrees register in crises through life. Progressions register in the years they denote. The Progressed Moon in a critical degree will register during that month.

CULMINATE: To complete the aim. A planet culminates when it reaches the highest point in the chart, the cusp of the 10th House or Midheaven, by either direct or converse motion. An aspect culminates when it reaches the exact degree required.

CUSP: The line marking the beginning of a house and also the point 30 minutes before the beginning of a Sign (so that a native is born "on the cusp", which is to say he exhibits some of the characteristics of both Signs and is often "on the fence").

DEBILITY: Weakening of a planet by being in its Fall or Detriment by Sign; peregrine, retrograde; afflicted in the 8th or 12th House; square or conjunct Mars or Saturn or besieged between them; in a critical degree or conjunct a malefic fixed star.

DECANATES: Parts of 10 degrees into which each Sign is divided. The first 10 degrees are of the nature of that Sign itself; the 2nd decanate has a sub-influence of the next Sign OF THE SAME ELEMENT (fire, earth, air or water). The 3rd decanate has a vibration of the final Sign of the same element.

DECLINATION: Distance north & south of the Celestial Equator. The Sun's greatest distance from the Celestial Equator is 23:27 degrees marking the Tropics of Cancer & Capricorn, the Solstice places where he turns to go back to the Celestial Equator. When leaving the Celestial Equator his declination increases; leaving Cancer & Capricorn it decreases.

DECREASING IN LIGHT: The Moon or a planet past the opposition of the Sun & now moving toward him. In horary, the matter asked about weakens & peters out to some extent. INCREASING IN LIGHT: The Moon or a planet past the conjunction of the Sun & moving away from him, empowered to develop favorably.

DETRIMENT: A planet in the Sign opposite to the one it rules and thus at a disadvantage because it has lost some power, which also affects the person it represents in the chart. It denotes incapacity to act in his own name, frustration and impediment in life: but if in mutual reception, the person is able to get around his difficulties later in life.

DIGNITY: This may be either Essential or Accidental. A planet in the Sign of its Dignity or its Exaltation, or same Element or in its own decanate is Essentially dignified & powerful. It is Accidentally dignified in any angular house, or the one it rules naturally (as Mars in the 1st or 8th), or if conjunct Jupiter or Venus or between them without the intervention of another planet; or when in mutual reception (giving it a secondary reading as though it changed places back to its own Sign).

DIRECTING: Another name for progressing when by a way different from the Secondary Method (p. 229). The Arc of Direction (page 217) added to a cusp or planet moves it forward to complete its aspect to another planet or cusp -- the Arc being the number of degrees between them, which also tells the age.

DISPOSE OF, DISPOSITS: The planetary ruler of a Sign in which another planet appears is called the dispositor of that other, displacing him in power. In horary, the person or thing represented by that disposited planet is in the power of another, who is empowered to dispose of him or it as he wishes. A planet in its own Sign shows by HOUSE where the native or horary querent will never be displaced.

DIURNAL: By day. Designating the upper half of the chart above the horizon, and including all the houses & planets there. NOCTURNAL: by night. The same thing for houses & planets below the horizon.

ECLIPSE: The darkening of the Sun or Moon while they are conjunct or opposition & near her nodes. The eclipse may be annular (a ring of darkness on the outer edge only) or partial (incomplete coverage) or total (complete coverage). The blacked-out symbol for the conjunction denotes a solar eclipse whose effects last 3 years or as many years as the eclipse lasted hours. The blacked-out opposition symbol denotes a lunar eclipse whose effects last 3 months or as many as the eclipse lasted hours.

ELECTION: A horary term for a chart set up for the best time elected (chosen) for an action to be taken under favorable lunar & planetary auspices.

ELEVATION: Highest position, as a planet in the 10th House or highest in the chart over the others so that it has "paramount" importance in the life.

ELONGATION: The greatest distance from the Sun that can be attained by either Mercury or Venus; about 28° for Mercury (p. 33) 48 for Venus (p. 41) therefore their aspects to him are very limited.

EPHEMERIS: A presentation of the planetary positions day by day (from ephemeral, or lasting only a day: transitory, therefore TRANSITS). Raphael's Ephemeris, which we use herein, is issued in booklet form for each year separately, giving the positions figured for noon and at Greenwich, England.

EQUATOR: An imaginary circle equating the globe dividing it into Northern & Southern Hemispheres. Extended into space, it is the Celestial Equator.

EXALTATION: The increased power of a planet in the Sign allotted to it as its Exaltation Sign, as the Sun in Aries. Such a person does his best work & rises to a higher position in the house it is in.

FALL: The weakened condition of a planet in the Sign opposite the one in which it is exalted. Such a person is capable of doing something calling for an apology - or demeaning himself in other's eyes.

FIGURE: Another name for the chart; also called a horoscope, nativity or geniture, scheme or map.

FORTUNA: The Arabian Point of Fortune. See page 133 for the Part of Fortune & Part of Mis-fortune.

FIXED SIGNS: Taurus, Leo, Scorpio and Aquarius.

FRUSTRATION: Prevention of a good aspect coming to fruition between two planets because a 3rd planet intervenes by a bad aspect to either of them. This is as strong in a natal chart as in a horary, breaking a promise or an engagement and preventing the person from following his own desires in life.

GENDER: The odd-numbered Signs are male and masculine in expression. The even-numbered Signs are female and feminine in expression. The native will express his individuality-Sun, personality-Moon, & temperament-Ascendant in the masculine or feminine way according to the gender of the Sign occupied. The Moon & Venus are feminine, the rest masculine. Mercury is dual by nature and susceptible to persuasion by Sign-gender. See CONVERTIBLE, p. 219.

GRAND ASPECTS: The trine becomes a Grand Trine when all three points are filled as Saturn in Leo, Mercury in Aries, and Jupiter in Sagittarius. The square becomes a Grand Square when all four points are filled as Mars in Taurus, Uranus in Leo, Venus in Scorpio and the Moon in Aquarius. When one of the points is not filled, the person is not understood in the house where the trine "falls out" and has difficulty in life where the square falls out.

HOUSES: The 12 sections into which the wheel or
chart is divided. The 1st, 4th, 7th & 10th Houses
are angular, indicating the angles of the chart as
well as the first house in each quadrant. Each is
followed by a succeedent house (the 2nd, 5th, 8th,
11th) which in turn is followed by a cadent house
(the 3rd, 6th, 9th & 12th) so that there is one of
each in each quadrant. More publicity comes to a
planet in an angular house, less in a succeedent &
still less in a cadent house which operates behind
the scenes as in service, teaching & broadcasting.

HYLEG: The Giver of Life - sometimes called the
Apheta as opposed to the Anareta or Taker of Life.
It has to do with a planet in a Hylegiacal place,
which can be from 5 degrees above the Ascendant to
25 degrees below, the same before & after the Descendant, and from 5 degrees before the 9th cusp to
25 below the 11th cusp. For a man, the Sun is hyleg in any of these places, otherwise the Moon.
For a woman the Moon is hyleg there, otherwise the
Sun. Lacking the Sun or Moon, the Ascendant is
taken as the Giver of Life for either man or woman.

IMMUM COELI (pronounced sée-ly). The Nadir, or
4th cusp; the "lower heavens". See MEDIUM COELI.

IMPEDE, IMPEDITED: Preventing from action. The
effect of a conjunction, square or opposition to a
significator, Ascendant, Sun or Moon involving the
malefics. The person will be held back by others.

INCREASING IN LIGHT: (See DECREASING IN LIGHT.)

INGRESS: To enter. Specifically, the chart set
for the Sun's entry into the Cardinal Signs Aries,
Cancer, Libra and Capricorn: it is read for world,
city and country news, conditions and developments
and whatever affects the president, king or ruler.

INTERCEPTED: Hemmed in. An intercepted Sign is one squeezed into a house whose restraining cusps show two other Signs: it is caused by another Sign appearing elsewhere on the cusps of two adjoining houses. An intercepted planet is one in an inter- cepted Sign. If at birth, it means lifelong threat of outside interference in matters governed by the house it is in, and specifically at the time it is under affliction. But if a progressed planet goes into an intercepted Sign, the native has gone into seclusion intentionally, withdrawing from others.

LATITUDE: Geographical distance north and south of the earth's equator. For the planets, distance north and south of the Sun's path. The Sun never has latitude. The wider the Moon's latitude which ordinarily does not exceed 5:18, the more latitude and scope the native takes in whatever he does.

LIGHTS: The luminaries (the Sun and the Moon).

LILITH: See SATELLITES herein. Her symbol is ⵁ

LONGITUDE: On earth, geographical distance east and west of Prime Meridian O-degrees at Greenwich. In the heavens, a planet's distance from O-degrees of the Sign it is in, as 0:02 Leo, 10 Aries, etc.

LUNATION: From Luna, the Moon: the conjunction, square or opposition between the Moon and Sun, but we usually mean only the New Moon conjunction: and the period from one New Moon to the next New Moon. The Full Moon finishes what the New Moon starts.

MALEFICS: Saturn-the-Reaper, Mars-the-Trouble- maker, Uranus-the-Disintegrator, Neptune-of-Fraud; Mercury if badly afflicted is a malefic in matters requiring signature, agreement or promise, such as contracts, examination papers, marriage & finance.

MALEFIC FIXED STARS: Caput Algol 24 Taurus, the
most evil of all; Serpentis 19 Scorpio the 'cursèd
degree of the accursèd Sign; the Ascelli 6 Leo and
Antares 8 Sagittarius affect the eyes; the Weeping
Sisters (the Pleiades 29 Taurus) give something to
weep about and thus also affect the eyes; and Vindemiatrix, Star of Widowhood, given as 8:41 Libra.

MEDIUM COELI (pronounced see-ly). The Zenith or
10th cusp, the M.C. or Midheaven. See IMMUM COELI.

MERIDIAN: Noon.   The 360 pole-to-pole lines of
distance around the earth, 1 degree apart & starting at 0-degrees, Greenwich, are called meridians.
24 of these are PRIME MERIDIANS, 15 degrees apart,
marking noon-time every hour on the hour somewhere
around the world.   Places that are not located on
a Prime Meridian call their line a LOCAL MERIDIAN.

MERIDIAN DISTANCE: The number of degrees between
a planet & its nearest meridian (10th or 4th cusp).

MIDHEAVEN: The highest point: Zenith, 10th cusp.

MOVABLE SIGNS (active, energetic): The Cardinal
Signs Aries, Cancer, Libra & Capricorn.   The Sun,
Moon & Mercury so placed show a changeable dispos-
ition; one too restless to stay long in one place.

MUNDANE: Worldly.   Involving the HOUSES of the
chart and the worldly matters they govern.   Also,
MUNDANE ASPECTS involving planets in aspect but by
house positions only, disregarding Sign and degree,
as Venus 10 Aries in the Third House is zodiacally
trine Mars 18 Leo in the Sixth House but square to
him by house, thus they are also in MUNDANE SQUARE.

MUTABLE SIGNS: Adaptable & adjustable to pressure: Common. Gemini, Virgo, Sagittarius, Pisces.

MUTE SIGNS: Cancer, Scorpio and Pisces, because they represent creatures that have no voice. They do not necessarily cause the person to be mute but they do denote a certain reticence and the ability to keep a secret or withhold some unsavory detail.

MUTUAL RECEPTION: Two planets in each other's natural Sign, as Sun in Cancer & Moon in Leo. It gives exchange status, as though back in their own Signs; and they may also be shown in color outside the wheel where their degrees would place them and given a secondary reading there. It means that the person can get out of what he gets into, or change places with someone else, compromise an otherwise-unsatisfactory arrangement and "return to normal".

NADIR: the 4th cusp, I.C., chart's lowest point.

NATIVITY: The natal chart. See FIGURE, p. 223.

NODES: The points where a planet's orbit crosses the ecliptic into north & south latitude mark its North & South Nodes, which change not more than $1\frac{1}{2}$ degrees in 100 years. Their N. Nodes in 1963 are:

Mercury - 18 Tau   Venus - 16 Gem   MOON given daily
Jupiter - 10 Can   Mars - 19 Tau   Saturn -- 20 Can
Neptune - 11 Leo   Pluto - 20 Can   Uranus -- 13 Gem

The South Node is the same degree & opposite Sign.

NORTHERN SIGNS: These are the first six Signs.

OCCULTATION: eclipse of a planet usually by Moon.

OBLIQUE ASCENDANT: The Arc of Direction gives the Directed Midheaven. Locate it in the Table of Houses & take its Ascendant for the birth latitude to use as the Obl/Asc with the Directed Ascendant.

OCCIDENTAL: West. On the Descendant side of the chart. OCCIDENTAL OF THE SUN: a planet following the Sun. In the natal chart, the Sun and Moon are occidental from the 4th to the 1st and also in the opposite quadrant. (See ORIENTAL, on this page.)

ORB: The leeway of a number of degrees allowed aspects that are approaching or leaving exactitude.

ORIENTAL: East. On the Ascendant side of the chart. ORIENTAL OF THE SUN: a planet rising ahead of the Sun. In a natal chart the Sun and Moon are oriental from the 1st to the 10th, and also in the opposite quadrant. (See OCCIDENTAL on this page.) Mercury "oriental of the Sun" denotes a native who looks before he leaps and always counts the cost.

PARALLEL OF DECLINATION: To be parallel, both planets may be in North Declination or both South, working like a conjunction as in holding together; or one in North Declination and the other in South Declination, threatening separation in the future.

PART OF FORTUNE: Formula: Ascendant plus Moon & then minus Sun. Fortuna represents the substance, good luck and improvement; and especially improved conditions in whatever is governed by the house in which it appears. It bestows more in Earth Signs.

PART OF MIS-FORTUNE: The Part of Fortune is the Part of Mis-fortune when in the 12th or 8th House or Pisces or Scorpio or a Pisces or Scorpio decanate, or conjunct Neptune or a malefic fixed star; in 29 degrees, or in the same degree as the nodes.

PARTILE: Degree-and-minute exactitude of aspect (but acceptable as partile even if the minutes are not close to exactitude). It increases importance. An aspect that is not exact is considered PLATIC.

PEREGRINE: Off base & wandering afar. Said of a planet (and the way it registers in natal & horary charts) when in a Sign in which it has no standing. A peregrine planet in the possession-2nd House or in any angular house warns of robbery and burglary.

PLATIC: An aspect not yet exact. (See PARTILE)

POSITED: Placed. As the Sun posited in the 3rd.

PROGRESSION: The forward movement of the cusps and planets in a chart. SECONDARY PROGRESSION is a method based on the new positions of the planets in the natal ephemeris; the 2nd day represents the second year, and so on. See p. 46, "Foundation of the Astrological Chart" for Secondary Progression, and p. 54 for the Radix Method called DIRECTING in which the ephemeris is discarded. (See DIRECTING)

PROHIBITION: Similar to FRUSTRATION (page 223). Where frustration may be temporary, prohibition is probably enduring, especially in certain horaries.

PROMITTOR: (prŏm-ittor). A planet that promises what it usually signifies under a good aspect that brings out its good side, or a bad aspect bringing out its bad side. Jupiter promises the cushioning flesh over our bones but under bad aspect he promises too much, resulting in obesity. Saturn promises desirable training under good aspect but when afflictive he promises undesirably-harsh and stern discipline. Mercury (the mind) and the Moon (the feelings & emotions) in good aspect are promittors of a sympathetic nature; if in bad aspect they are inclined towards coldness in expressing affection, sympathy or generosity in the early part of life.

QUADRANTS: The four sections into which a wheel (the chart) is divided by the horizon and meridian.

QUARTILE: Another name for the 90-degree square.

QUERENT: The person who asks a horary question.

QUESITED: The person or thing (or matter) asked about in a horary question, signified by the ruler of the house that covers the question. If it is a thing, the planet naturally ruling it is included as co-significator (Mercury-papers, Venus-purses).

RADICAL: means that the chart is correct insofar as the data & mathematics are concerned: readable.

RADIX: The birth chart. RADIX SYSTEM OF DIRECT-ING: progressing the cusps and planets by age-arc.

RECTIFICATION: Correction of the hour of birth, done through the Midheaven's degree. (See p. 66)

REFRANATION: To refrain from acting. When one of the planets in an aspect either leaves the Sign it is in or turns retrograde before the aspect can be completed, so that no further action is taken.

RETROGRADE: Backward in the Sign. Denotes illness, shyness, more in the case than meets the eye.

RIGHT ASCENSION: Distance from 0-Aries measured along the Celestial Equator: used in Primary Arcs.

RISING SIGN: The Sign on the Ascendant. If not Aries, it brings "to the fore" whatever it usually represents temperamentally, as well as the matters and persons of the house where it normally belongs.

SATELLITES: Moons. The earth has a second satellite, Lilith, called the dark moon of the earth because seen only by her shadow as she crosses the face of the Sun. (Page 1, "The Dark Moon Lilith")

SATELLITIUM: A group of planets in one Sign.

SEPARATION: The onward "separating" motion of a faster planet leaving an aspect. See APPLICATION.

SIDEREAL TIME: The distance within 24:00:00 degrees traveled by the Sun each year at an approximate daily increase of four minutes, and starting two days after the Vernal Equinox on March 21st. Note that the ephemeris gives the Sun's Sign and degree each day & its equivalent in Sidereal Time.

SIGNIFICATOR: The planet representing the querent or quesited in a horary chart. If not usable, the Moon substitutes and is named CO-SIGNIFICATOR.

SIGNS: The twelve 30-degree sections of the 360° circle (which is the ecliptic or Sun's path) named Aries, Taurus, Gemini, Cancer, Leo, Virgo, Libra, Scorpio, Sagittarius, Capricorn, Aquarius & Pisces.

SOLSTICE SIGNS: Cancer & Capricorn, marking the Sun's greatest distance from the Celestial Equator. SOLSTICE POINT: A planet's distance from 0-Cancer or 0-Capricorn, whichever it is nearer, taken the same distance across to the other side. The planet's remaining degrees in the Sign it is in are the degrees for its Solstice Point.   Use the Sign on the same line with it in this writer's diagram:

Capricorn	:	Sagittarius
Aquarius	:	Scorpio
Pisces	:	Libra
Aries	:	Virgo
Taurus	:	L e o
Gemini	:	Cancer

Mars in 14:58 Aquarius (from 29:60) shows his S.Pt Scorpio 15:02 (these Signs being on the same line).

SPHERE: A circle. The Terrestrial Sphere is the earth; the Celestial Sphere the heavens. The Sun, Moon, stars & planets are spheres. The sphere of a planet is its orbit; man's sphere is his lifetime.

STATION, STATIONARY: Planets changing direction are between being one way or the other - such as a person at a station en route somewhere. They are STATIONARY (at a standstill, waiting) and marked S.

STELLIUM: A group of stars. (See SATELLITIUM)

SUCCEEDENT: Following an angular house, as the 2nd, 5th, 8th and 11th. They are financial houses whose cusps are the crosslines in Fortuna's symbol.

SYNTHESIZING THE CHART: Taking everything into consideration in delineating the chart as a whole.

TABLE OF HOUSES: A list of Signs and degrees to write on the cusps of the houses in the chart.

TESTIMONY: A position or aspect in the chart of importance in confirming the reading or judgment.

TRANSIT: To pass over. Said of planets in the current ephemeris as they pass over (conjunct) the natal or progressed planets in the chart. The opposition is equally striking in effect, especially if an eclipse, in an angle, or involving malefics.

TRINE OF THE CHART: A line drawn from the 10th to the 2nd to the 6th & back to the 10th forms the trine of the chart, usually giving all in the same element, making for a more balanced pattern. But sometimes an intercepted Sign in the chart throws one of these cusps out of element so that the pattern in life is upset. It may denote money or possessions, health or tenancy, employment or career.

TRIPLICITY: The Signs in threes of the same element, as the Fire Triplicity (Aries, Leo & Sagittarius), the Earth, the Air and Water Triplicity.

TROPICAL SIGNS: Cancer & Capricorn, $23°26'37.87''$ North & South of the Celestial Equator marking the limits of the Torrid Zone where the Sun turns (the meaning of tropic) back to the Celestial Equator.

UNDER THE SUNBEAMS: Within 17 degrees before or after the Sun & not necessarily in the same Sign. It is mildly upsetting, denoting timidity, fear or stage-fright putting the person at a disadvantage.

UNFORTUNATE SIGNS: Taurus, Cancer, Virgo, Scorpio, Capricorn and Pisces, especially when rising, are said to give a tendency to misfortune in life, or to counteract some of the good fortune enjoyed.

VIA COMBUST WAY: A fiery-star section between 15 Libra and 15 Scorpio, rendering a significator there as ineffectual as when COMBUST the Sun (within 8½ degrees before or after him, but only in the same Sign); the only safe place being the benefic star Spica's in 22/23 Libra. A person described by a planet via combust encounters misfortune in life.

VIOLENT SIGNS: Aries, Scorpio, Capricorn & frequently Aquarius because ruled by malefic planets.

VOID OF COURSE: A planet making no applying aspect from the Sign it is in (especially the horary Moon, denoting no activity to expect because going nowhere & doing nothing). In a natal chart it has a milder influence applied to the Moon, describing the person as less sensitive, more sanguine regarding life in general, poised & with inner assurance and more self-reliance: a calm & more mature soul.

* * * * *